ORAL TRADITION

-

IN AFRICAN LITERATURE

Smith and Ce [ed.]

AFRICAN
Library of Critical Writing

ORAL TRADITION - in African Literature
©Smith and Ce (Eds.)

©African Library of Critical Writing
Print Edition
ISBN:978-9-7836-0359-2

Formatted for print and electronic [e-pub and e-content] editions by Handel Books Ltd.
For information address please write:
Progeny (Press) International
Attn: African Books Network
9 Handel Str.
AI EBS Nigeria WA
Email: handelbooks@yandex.com

Marketing and Distribution in the US, UK,
Europe, N. America (Canada),
and Commonwealth countries by
 African Books Collective Ltd.
PO Box 721
Oxford OX1 9EN
United Kingdom
Email: orders@africanbookscollective.com

Contents

Chat

Chapter 8

Notes and Bibliography

Introduction

THE publication by Amos Tutuola of his novel The Palm Wine Drinkard in 1952 brought to the fore the rich pool that oral traditions of Africa offered for writers who recognised its vast potential for the creative enterprise. Yet it was The African Child by Laye Camara, in 1953, which placed the griot in a central creative profession that brings history, tradition, culture and literacy in their fullest intersections with African education. And with the publication of Chinua Achebe's Things Fall Apart, in 1958, and Arrow of God, in 1964, the rich traditional heritage of the African world found its most dynamic expression in serious literary engagement.

While much studies have been made of the oral repertoire, and its significance for modern writing by literary scholars, attempts to maintain a one dimensional study of oral craft have not yielded the desired coherent and contemporaneous application of orality to literature. Ironically, the study of oral literature as a genre existing on its own terms and structures and formulae has only tended to place the traditions in pristine isolation from contemporary literary developments. Regrettably, oral studies (orature) have waned on the syllabi of many

African universities as the written form seems to eclipse the oral space.

Our commitment to the study in oral traditions is borne from the awareness that African verbal arts still survive in works of discerning writers, and in the conscious exploration of its tropes, perspectives, philosophy and consciousness, its complementary realism, and ontology, for the delineation of authentic African response to memory, history and all possible confrontations with modern existence such as witnessed in recent analyses of the African novel. These studies use multi-faceted theories of orality which discuss and deconstruct notions of history, truth-claim, identity-making, genealogy (cultural and biological), and gendered ideologies.

In this series we have strived to adopt innovative and multilayered perspectives on orality or indigeneity and its manifestations on contemporary African and new literatures. Here therefore is an important contribution which integrates the oral traditions of African writing within new and relevant contemporary expressions through exploring the literary permutations of oral traditional performance in the works of several African writers.

Ce and Smith

Chapter 1

Re-visioning African Writing

C. Ce

THERE are times that we are constrained to admit to ourselves that sparing the bright chap literatures of Southern Africa's liberation writings in a fictional or life writing sense to 'tell the truth' about the experiences of real people or situations (Coullie 7) the best of our writing are pale products of African art because they struggle as facsimiles of real or imagined hegemonic Western traditions. It remains uncertain, however, how many living authors and critics would concede some praise for the new poetics that must discard this aging school that foisted imitative craft and visioning on African writing as some bold critics and revisionists of the canons had tried to show.

It is now a long time ago when this seed of handicap was laid in African writing, probably unwittingly, in the overtures of our 'modern' writers and critics. These were Africa's Western educated men and women who, faced with the singular evidence of purposive aesthetics in the hierarchy of communal values, turned to vaunted Grecian celebrities and celebrators of human moral disfigurement. Maybe this was because they were obligated, in Palmer's terms, to convince readers of the realism of the world being presented (4) or amuse them with the sterile voyeurism of imperial cultures. But a few have preferred that we chart an alternate, clearer vision for African writing–with the impetus of its historical cultural specifics–which requires that one must needs recover some flickering remnants of arcane light (ancestral wisdom) for a further enlightened posterity.

The supposition for a reassessment of cultural direction from a firmly rooted indigenous structure took strong roots long before projects such as "the independent propagation of African thought and aesthetics"1 and the famous decolonisation treatises by some Afrocentric scholars2 along with the work of poets, statesmen and visionaries, began to turn their backs at the formations of theory, philosophy and education along frequently racial- and language-dominant paradigms.

At the close of his autobiographical series in A Dream of Africa Camara Laye had inserted an injunction to fellow African writers:

Never forget the enemy is not a race… but a gang of profiteers. Fight against that gang; entrust your country to reliable men, to men who have already shown their mettle: then you will open the gates of your country to the entire world, to all the intelligence and expertise that may be found among all the peoples of the world, to all those qualities that urge people to conquer everything in the domains of the intellect, of art, of technology.3

Here Laye's idea of conquest does not quite imply the Darwinian evolutionist survival of the fittest but in the light of 'conquest' as transcending human limitations and a recognition of one's role in the spiritual, material and teleological order of a more expansive universe –an excellent premise of most African and Asian cultural traditions.

In advanced cultures the simple ending of many story telling, 'to live happily ever after', has been perceived by a learned and sophisticated literati not in the context of that persistence that is seen in smaller parts reaching to merge with their whole and highest ideals or that which drives people in forward-moving aspiration beyond their various limitations but as products of artistic and visionary naiveté. But if chauvinists of modern literature would look deeper into tradition and culture and, as Clement supposes, into such stories as those that taught "the history of man" and showed "exactly what is meant by the word 'history'"(13) they will find in them an ancient premise where the finest thread of evil is altered, although never absolutely voided, by the greater, yet never simplistic or exclusively traditional, good. Such undying motifs of a wholistic order in the universe suppose the need for conquest in the unifying sense of parts reaching for their whole. These are partly embedded in African oral narratives and visual arts although only as a constant motif within some confused and mutant variants.

Why was it that in cultures of the twentieth and twenty-first centuries modern African writing came to be calcified in the so called realism or realistic fiction and still remains the winning mind-set for many a creative literary and critical endeavour? Was it rather to conceive of the appropriate predicament, of inexhaustible malevolence and the scientific reduction of humans as self seeking material entities who must conquer the known and unknown before them, that the modern order had proffered a reality of failure, disorder and turbulence within the parts of the greater whole? This reality thus created found a vent in eternal paradoxes befitting of a people's fragmented existence. Was this supposed to vindicate men's paucity of moral strength or feebleness in the face of definite evil, a tragic reality finding evidence in slavery, feudalism, imperialism, the world wars and their similar replications among pockets of lesser nation states? If probably true how then do we extract the sickness of the human condition from literary creativity and serious imaginative fiction?

In a healthy criticism of emerging canons Achebe in 'Africa and her Writers' passed off Armah's novel, The Beautyful ones are not yet born, as "sick with the sickness of the human condition" (25). Arrow of God was similarly deprecated for its "dogged secularisation of the profoundly mystical" (91) by Soyinka who took a critical step in Myth, Literature and the African World to spell an alternate compass for navigating Africa's mythological heritage. Now that disapprobation of Armah's 'existentialism' by Achebe will sound very much like the proverbial pot calling the kettle black especially when the latter's quixotic attachment to his tragedies is seen in the context of most, if not all, of his novels as Obi enthuses in No Longer at Ease:

Real tragedy is never resolved. It goes on hopelessly for ever. Conventional tragedy is too easy. The hero dies and we feel a purging of the emotions. A real tragedy takes place in a corner, in an untidy spot, to quote W. H. Auden. The rest of the world is unaware of it. Like that man in A Handful Dusts who reads Dickens to Mr. Todd. There is no release for him. When the story ends he is still reading. There is no purging of the emotions for us because we are not there. (36)

Vestiges of Aristotelian foundation in Western aesthetics coming into our world should have witnessed a few permutations if not straight redundancy or worse each time we recall a more ancient, ethically rooted, and pre-Socratic tradition that is scrupulous about substance of stories upheld by society (Griffith 360). For truly conscious writers and their readers, since Ancient Egypt and Greece, did often interrogate the value and merit of that which is unleashed on the local communion. Though the creative literary exercise in modern Africa, especially poetry, is deemed a "ritual communion in which the expression of oneness is self-evident and out of which a new awareness is inevitable" (Vincent 'Intro'), the welter of expression has lacked an indigenous theoretical compass by which they are anchored. The tendency has been the replication of European and American paradigms which overlooks an overarching and preponderant traditional or oral heritage. Traditional aesthetic, an intrinsic part of African communal heritage, should act much more on recent creative expressions as a solid influence, a characteristic of expression that lends a stamp of cultural identity to the literary genre in which it subsists, and which is Platonian in the sense of its inscription of "the worth of ultimate reality as spiritual" (Bressler 12). Its linking of literature and life (politics) in a "moral and reasoned worldview" is the concern, nay, the "value, nature and worth of the artist and of literature itself" (13).

Nowadays despite that the two greats of African writing namely Achebe and Soyinka had in their respective ways, doctored the indulgence of younger writers and propagated some beneficent artistic alternatives from many possible theoretical points of view, we may be spurred by the gift of hindsight to assess the argument in the light of knowledge regarding our universe and our relationships within our heritage.

In our literary circle a revision is overdue; it hardly needs to be argued again that even No Longer at Ease had betrayed the same self-defeating surrender to inexorable moral and ethical corruption –and ultimate death of an ideal– as The Beautyful Ones are not yet born. Perhaps that song in Achebe's novel: "he that has a brother must hold him to heart" (117) artistically backgrounds the determined clamour of Umuofia town union to bail their kinsman and so brings that tragic repast closer to native wisdom of transcendent kindred compassion as a beholden ideal. But we might argue that this was also demonstrated by the nameless man of Armah's story who helps his corrupt neighbour to flee political vendetta during a wave of some suspect revolutionary insurgence. The difference, as always, is in the writer's purpose and vision for his art.

Inclusive of the African writer's tendency to pessimism was Ngugi's own disenchantment with

18

Capitalist civilisation, his absorption of modernist Marxist ideology and the presumption of its replication in our present world sense. Further again most or all of Munonye's, Amadi's and Emecheta's novels were afflicted, to varying degrees of notoriety, by Western materialistic perceptions of social and personal tragic fortunes and other values of creative and literary execution not readily reconciled with a counter-balancing African spiritual landscape for which Achebe himself had championed gruesomely against the 'colonialist criticism' that trailed his early novels. It probably explains why Amadi's Concubine, by characterisation and execution, lost the configuration of African womanhood in Ihuoma but capitulated to the pedantry of tragic fate: the idea of man "caught in webs and mysteries he cannot understand, (or) explain" or from which he may never "disentangle" (Eko 34) and by this slippery fall blinded a rather exhilarating development of character and personality in one of our cerebral African heroines.

Our having to toe in Occidental greatness also included Munonye's perfect Grecian inspirational story of the 'Oil man'3 whose existence, while suspended in tragic destiny, repulsed his human triumph over a Sisyphean curse that must dog his life. For had not the realism of Things Fall Apart and Arrow of God given rise, or at least consolidated, ideas of tragic degeneracy and foggy visions of a Soyinkan 'wasted breed' overwhelmed by the conspiracy and powerful consort of devilry such as had merited a poetry book dedication in our mid nineties to "many others wallowing in the futility of existence" (iv) - this by no less a product of the old school than Chris Nwamuo.

Carried away by the reconstruction of the colonial and neo-colonial experience African writing may have lost the pantheon of spirits which imbued order and balance to life, rallied round men and women to affirm their mettle because they always said, and acted, in some purposive spiritual direction. This is in spite of its pragmatic universe that endowed a man the maker of his own fortune and guided him in the recognition of the positive presence of his gods -a world view which corollary can be expressed as tenets of the diligence to own those "acres of diamonds"(58) which Conwell had told his fellow Americans was within their reach if only they could learn to look deep enough around their various domiciles. Ours was also an ontology that Achebe reminded us would so spurn fatalism and absolutism to the extent that the created would talk and bargain with its creator at those nebulous processes of evolution to arrive at a reasonable compromise prior to an earthly incarnation ("Chi" 103).

Somehow the moral virtue that had endeared men and women to their ancient earthly bond and their communal responsibilities in extension were hardly found on a generous scale in the literary imagination of what we may now call the writings of the moderns. It had appeared that the dominant questions of complex modern conditions had stampeded a man's Chi to continue to say nay in spite of his high and lofty affirmations. And having chosen the dictum of artistic realism with, perhaps, but little interrogation of reality shifts which often found expression in the hardly-reconciled oppositions of modern existence the ultimate mastery that is presumed beyond all human attainments was bound in negligent or vicious abuse. Thus did we inherit a Pandora's Box of social or moral burden, one in which the elements and that great sin are in a grand conspiracy to foist failure upon humankind keeping them eternally blinded in their aspirations, a step beyond their ken. It sounds in line with that mystery that loses its fanciful attractiveness or "familiar sense of wonder" once "innocence departs and knowledge settles in" as Achebe tells of Tangayinka (77). How so true of our political and economic predicaments!

We have been rather fortunate that the old fox of African literature was later to attend to a few helpful insights regarding the dissatisfactory execution of some of his writing although he had earlier chosen to spurn 'colonial housewives' and critics who felt that he ought to have conceded a nobler ending for that Clara-Obi romance. So in Anthills of the Savannah, coming in the beautiful eighties of our literary revisions, we are gratuitously offered Beatrice and Elewa as symbols of maternal redemption, the modern implantation of a genetic code that will confront tyranny and the corruptive degeneracy of society in their entire ramifications. In spite of this distinction our foray in those Anthills still leaves the lachrymal aftertaste of an eternal tragedian's recipe.

The frustration of heroes in their bid to carry through an ideal and, in extension, seize the opportunities of their age, was for African writers a mad run to some centuries of European literary traditions or, for Rotimi and Osofisan, the mythological interpolation of an original past that must still be juxtaposed with its Orphic or Sophoclean parallels. It has also seemed that Nwapa,

Emecheta, and even our good sister Aidoo have been too much of pessimists in undoing the real heroes of their societies. For there were, and still are, men and women in real life who, much like Moremi in Osofisan's Morotoudon, successfully defied our social conspiracies - the useless osu system of the Igbo race for instance- and still lived out their positive destinies of greatness in their own right. Arguably the otherwise gloomy resolutions of the old school did not help and thus were truly not on the side of the many other dispossessed and disinherited of our African earth in spite of every claim to progress and commitment on their part. For what modern society truly required in the blank white days of colonial treachery and its aftermaths were more of the stories of a few good men (great stories that rear to inspire all generations) who challenged the negativity engrafted upon our routine thoughts and fashions to dare any listener to those eternal values and conditions that humans must strive to resolve.

Unfortunately scarcely interrogated influences dig into Africa because of an elitist education that persists in a wholesale adoption of foreign traditions and other intellectual and theological affiliations of the Western world that are presently set to implode in their own gross materiality and falsehood. Only from a bohemian approach to his characters which we see realised in a Jero or Sanda4 and his redeployment of tribal history and mythology, such as the horseman and his progeny's fulfilment of an ancient ritual, does Soyinka leave us some of his most imaginative literary creations thus offering a glimmer of light to a generation benumbed in modernist contempt for the beleaguered of society. Olunde5 becomes a parable for human subordination of the separate, selfish existence for the moral and ethical elevation of society and all sacrificing beings of light. Yet even as a protestation for the mystical experience or the articulation of an indigenous alternative via historical mythologising Ogunism soon grew inadequate for the interpretation of an African and Diasporic existence with its propositions readily wearing along popular Jungian and other vertiginous archetypes intended to illuminate the cul-de-sac of realist art. Which meant finding ourselves in want of further vision.

So intensely are the conditions of realist cynicism ingrained in Africa's westernised elites that current academic reading of African fictions might readily bow to its frenzied permutations. With the proposition to mark the beginnings of modernism in African literature with The Palm Wine Drinkard (Nnolim 64) the sorry prospect of this second-fiddle academics is that younger researchers are tempted to start a reading of literary modernist theories in narratives which do not fit eighteenth century traditions of European story-telling. Now the exploration of the supernatural worlds resplendent and majestic in African fictional memory may then become instances of modernist, magical-realism which have seen a few young African writers as adherents. And the tradition of story telling in Africa with its blend of contemporary experience, its latitude for wider artistic individuality as against imitative notions, its pristine aesthetic motifs, fluidity, spirituality and experimentation will be subsumed in one pet box of Western nomenclature.

If African writing should incline in the frenzied direction of theory and taxonomy it will be forcing itself into more blurring compartments that always have Europe's and America's closed guess-works as exemplars of literary, cultural and philosophical directions. But somehow a state must be the product of individual citizens whose characters can trace back to the state's own sense of history and progress. Which makes an abiding literary ideal behove of the need to interrogate actions and thoughts of the few men, women, children, and even animals or situations, whose purport to represent collective values and individual aspirations meets ingenious artistic executions.

A few decades ago the world of Laye Camara or Senghor was deemed rather "too sweet"5 for our moderns. But a future generation, worried by an absence on the part of her writers of ideal insights and plausible imaginative constructs of our expanding universe may well look to the sweet world and craft of The Dark Child for some helpful liberation from the vice grip of absolute pessimism. And they may probably concede to Camara that appellation of the most visionary artiste to come out of Africa. For The Radiance of the King is not just about a disreputable European or The Dark Child and A Dream of Africa some whims of Negritude romanticism. These are but affiliates of the imaginative re-validation of past and future directions by which African peoples and, by extension, other beleaguered members of the world's wastelands may plod their course.

We should be glad that some writers of the eighties are not quite like the fifties and sixties generation -or older members of their own generation if we align with Hermetic thought to concede forty years for generational shifts. Those little-sung writings of the eighties such as witnessed in some works of Okoye, Ba, Okpewho and Ezeigbo6 were marks of positive revisionism in the sense that they sought an end to the fleeting palliatives of methodically Westernised influences through avid arguments directed against their symptoms wherever they foisted themselves in the remote reaches of our thought. With practice millennial writing may still shed remnant notions of progress and history borrowed from imperial worlds blighted by greed and prejudice. This has come in light of other interpretations of reality breaking upon our sleeping intellectual and cosmological traditions. In this process all hemispheres, Eastern and Western, would have brought some light to bear on centuries of medieval Western cosmology impacting its backwardness on scientific, historical, religious and literary engagements.

Many centuries after Darwinian and Newtonian popular traditions the world should be glad in the knowledge that some of the Judeo-Christian theologies and their myths which grafted ages of darkness upon the world are being upstaged by more plausible constructs of human advancement or regression through millennia of history. No doubt other hypotheses than Velikovsky's7 must be set to further convulse our world in the years ahead. More original theories of human civilisation suppressed by theological prejudices may be collaborated beyond mere speculations to enliven human knowledge and bring mis-interpreted mysteries of so-called primitive peoples away from the contempt and prejudice of clandestine religious interests.

Here now lies the challenge of foresight for African literary or linguistic enquiries and future creative experimentation. It is the illumination of ancestral wisdom by the imaginative revelation of the greater unity in the diversities that are embedded in our external and subjective realities. This was something which our arcane forebears knew then to be apparent in the universe to wit their proverbial 'wisdom like a goatskin bag,'8 unique in individualised perceptions, yet central to the very complex and challenging nature of expanding reality. We can grant that the dawn of fictional belle letters and the allowing for their appreciation by a bold and courageous literati will result in even more fascinating interpretations of the truths and aesthetics of our existence.

A re-vision of African writing demands that we play down the vocal coterie of voices bemused and magnetised, like our political leaders, with the commercialism, internationalism and abject materialism of Europe and America if only to pay heed to our own bold voice directed by a purpose to grant individual and audience respite from replications of viral failures, not to talk of worn fads that concede endemic malaise as the ultimate undertaking in realism and its "magical" equivalents. The new literatures should come to accept the possibility of an order in which space and existence are seen for their varying and changing dimensions which can readily be negotiated by random application of the mind's eye to thought, and by deeper enquiries that change and shape social conditions, thereby holding out pleasant surprises in the discovery of an amazing residue of possibilities.

This may not be the amazing kind of street side literature exemplified in Ngugi's latest experiment with bulk. For Wizard of the Crow as interpreted from Gikuyu to English is still a successive muzzling of the promise of earlier work and smacks of that crude overkill that has Osofisan's Reore gloating that "there is no other gods but our muscles" (85). The ideological coliseum that has tyranny and conquest in confrontation with resistance and subversion -all in that Manichaean chaos- seems now like a tame lion, more of an idiosyncrasy that must be shown to be distinct from fidelity of artistic visioning, the soul of craft.

In Southern African writing, for a change, it is good that in spite of the seemingly endless answering or talking backs, their women's voice-throwing ("Shades" 13) is moving on to anchor on the truly original individual and collective experience. This African progress consists in looking inwards, attuning and employing the benefits of the environment in understanding the function of the greater whole and our continental role within its constructs. For the literary tour de force that will gloss over plausible history within the progression of individual and collective existence, being the discovery of what we truly are, and where we are headed in a positively expanding sense, may well concede its lack of purpose in any African or universal scheme of letters.

Africa has had ancient works of dynamic and meaningful universal affiliations within original and wholistic individualities. This is in spite of all the loud and fashionable opinions that emphasise the converse. It speaks very little now of our generation that for several decades after our colonisation and exploitation we still await clear, fresh and inward looking and community-relevant, expressions which ought to have sustained our early modern literary and critical schema. That there should include truly original perspectives which pride in knowing the past, interpreting the present and exploring the future from fidelity to our cultural endowments, rational vigour and sense of positive destiny means that when this finally becomes a constant in the literary engagement of art with community, we would have entered an era of enlightenment of which any previous renaissance was only a shadowy precursor and in which the future is its welcome harbinger.

Issues in Oral Tradition

Chapter 2

The Folktale in Achebe's Fictions

Roy, Anjali G. "Telling Africa in the Manners of Folk: Chinua Achebe." Perspectives on African Literatures at the Millennium. Eds. Drayton, Arthur D., Omofolabo Ajayi-Soyinka and I. Peter Ukpokodu (Trenton NJ: Africa World Press), 2006.

A Gera Roy

THANKS to the pioneering efforts of Ruth Finnegan, Emmanuel Obiechina, Bernth Lindfors, Isidore Okpewho and others, African orature studies have grown into a highly specialized discipline.1 A comparison of early studies with those appearing later shows how the ethno-text becomes increasingly specific as it is redefined first, in national, and then, in regional terms.2 Studies of orature in Nigerian fiction have drawn on multidisciplinary perspectives for various purposes such as the identification of individual folklore items, the use of folklore as a structuring strategy, and more recently, to focus on the oral-written interface. However, they continue to ascribe to African orature the same functions that folklore borrowings have performed in Western literatures. If we recall the oppositional role of orality in post-colonial resistance, African orature cannot afford to replicate Western trends. Far from contributing to their novels' anthropological flavour or acting as symbolic devices, folk materials revise the anthropological discourse of the West through which African cultures were inferioritized. They do so by juxtaposing an alternative idiom–of African orature–with its own unique manner of structuring reality that might offer a way of ending Africa's discursive indentureship to the West.

However, to suggest that African oratures reflect an 'oral-aural' world at odds with the worlds created by literacy is to repeat Western anthropology's essentialist fallacy that, it is hoped, will be avoided here. Anthropologists such as Levy Bruhl and Horton attempted to provide a systematic description of the differences between traditional and modern thought systems. Levy Bruhl labeled preliterate mythic systems as prelogical because, according to him, they do not possess the rule-governed outlook of the modern. His notion of "mystical participation" in describing traditional cultures presupposed that they believe in propositions that are "intrinsically incoherent". Similarly, Horton used five interlinked categories–unreflective, unsystematic, with mixed motives, having low cognitive division of labour and protective attitude to beliefs and concepts–tried to interpret traditional systems for the Western mind.5 However, as these descriptions are made within the discourse of the modern Western, they reflect the concerns and classifications of the modern. The tendency of the traditional mind to personalize non-human forces and its preference for a mystical explanation strikes the Western rational mind as prelogical or irrational. But as

Levy Bruhl himself conceded later, the prelogical attitudes he located in traditional thought was as characteristic of modern science in areas it sought to interpret phenomena.6 In certain kinds of propositions, namely the atomic, belief plays as large a role as in traditional systems.

The non-literate and literate are, therefore, not mutually exclusive worlds but different languages become clear as Nigerian fiction systematically works to expose the fallacies of Western anthropology. To begin with, it strikes at the essentialism in the binary division of literate and preliterate worlds. As new evidence of the presence of writing in Africa is brought to light, the myth of a purely preliterate Africa ceases to be true.7 While the variables along which orality and literacy are split are themselves contestable, their hierarchization has no basis in fact. Even if one grants that preliterate societies are prelogical, nonrational and governed by mystical explanation as it was alleged, there is an implicit valorization of the logical\rational and scientific understanding as the Western Self privileges its own categories. If one goes a step further, one realizes that orality appears as it does in written discourses because it is defined through the categories of writing.

The Nigerian novel records the process by which the imposition of categories of writing distorts African orality. As an African oral universe is reflected through written filters, their role in othering Africa becomes evident. This process can be seen at work in the much discussed final paragraph of Things Fall Apart as the shift to the anthropological register reduces the heroic legend of Okonkwo into a paragraph about a quaint native custom.8 The entire anthropological discourse of modernity through which Africa was either written out of history and civilization or marginalized to a footnote is invoked in this masterly conclusion. If the entire novel reads this discourse oppositionally in Things Fall Apart, Arrow of God alternates Igbo passages with those in Standard English to underline how a shift in filters radically alters the content.9 In Achebe's urban novels, the westernized Nigerians unwittingly reiterate the anthropological perspective in their approach to oral African heritage, which is offset by vestigial oral voices. Soyinka's westernized protagonists share the limitations of interpreting the Nigerian past through non-western eyes. While the university-educated writer cannot replicate Tutuola's semi-literate sensibility and must distance himself from his oral materials, he does project the oral as a self-contained episteme ruled by its own classification systems. It is important to note that this oral language is not upheld as superior or inferior but different from the rational scientific. Whether Okonkwo's act of killing Ikemefuna is given a mystical explanation—an offence against a goddess or condemned as an inhuman act in the language of liberal humanism, the nature of the act does not alter in any substantive manner. The history of racism, on the other hand, is predicated on the privileging of one kind of explanation over the other. Post-colonial Nigerian fiction preserves the difference in modes of perception; but it jettisons the hierarchy.

However, in Western anthropology's collecting African folklore to interpret African culture negatively as well as post-colonial revisionism's falling back on the same device to enunciate African cultural difference is the recognition of orature as a cultural code.

Though Levi Strauss viewed myth as a semiotic system reflecting preliterate cultural priorities promoted the metaphorical mode as a counterpoint to the scientific, he did not escape the paternalistic Western mindset. In equating mythic with scientific knowledge by calling myth as the science of the concrete, he unconsciously imposed alien taxonomies that dissolved their difference.10 According scientific status to mythic modes is to introduce alien categories for scientific logic appears, not just antithetical, but irrelevant to the epistemic frame of orality. Nigerian fiction, therefore, does not seek to legitimize oral mores and belief through an appropriation of scientific reasoning. It is content to let them remain in their indigenous epistemic frames.

If objects and facts are intelligible only in terms of the world horizons they belong to, the reader must be made to recognize that details of African lives become intelligible only against the backdrop of the African world. One must remember that the alien reader needs to be initiated into the African episteme and cosmology to approach the African material with insiders' perspective. Since the novels deal with material deeply embedded in the African cosmos, material that has been distorted beyond recognition by imperial representations, the novelists must provide the reader with an appropriate code for deciphering his stories. Studies of language in Nigerian fiction relating its use of non Standard to indigenous modes of perception draw on the idea that linguistic filters mediate reality often, which can be carried over to the novel's incorporation of orature. If orature is viewed as a language, a system of signs, it becomes clear how the language of myth, folktale, proverbs, oratory, ritual and prayers construct the African world of the imperial text differently. As African writing negotiates a terrain unfamiliar to the novel reader, or one that has been estranged through Western representations, the writer is obliged to provide those signposts that can help the reader comprehend these worlds in the manner their inhabitants perceive them. It is true that the alien reader does not require additional background information to understand the novels because orature provides these signposts, a theory for reading the Nigerian novel.11 It is also part of the Nigerian writer's strategy for supplementing the Western novel's bourgeois filters with indigenous ones.

Though traditionally folklore studies have conceded the status of orature as a cultural code, they have cited folklore to inferiortize folk cultures. Folklore becomes the site of the 'primitive's lack of culture as well as of the construction of the child/native analogy. However, citing folklore—dubbed childlike stories and songs of childish people—as a further illustration of the 'primitive's' lack of civilization ignores its original function. While entertainment might have been part of the folklore agenda, orature has been recognized as a means of codifying folk wisdom and has functioned as the main pedagogic tradition in non-literate societies. It is appropriate that Achebe should not only enjoin a teaching function on the African writer but also resort to teaching in the same manner that African people have always taught. And it is not surprising that, in the absence of writing, gnomic traditions should have embodied the collective wisdom of non-literate cultures. But evidence of the continuity of these traditions, even in societies in possession of a script demonstrates an attachment to oral modes of transmitting knowledge that is seen to be lost in writing. One of the earliest examples of this tradition, the Indian Panchtantra collected employs the oral mode to teach practical wisdom.12 The tale of the Panchatantra's composition, of the Brahmin Visnusarma who took up the challenge of educating the three daft sons of King Amarshakti by telling them stories, highlights the pedagogic function of folklore. The fact that Panchatantra appeared long after the acquisition of literacy in India makes it possible for the frame tale to contrast the pedagogic methods of orality and literacy. If literacy has engendered formal systems of instruction culminating in the institution of schooling whose exclusionary machinery commodifies both writing and learning, orature as an informal instruction system requires no paraphernalia. Visnusarma's innovative learning method separates mere book learning from buddhiprabodham, the awakening of the intellect that will equip the princes with the practical skills for living in the real world. Non-literate instruction methods use life as their textbook, presenting real life problems in the guise of stories, riddles, songs and proverbs that delight as well stimulate of the listener.14 The difference between the two is that while the bardic tradition transmits both cultural and natural information, even fully literate societies depend on oral modes for transmitting certain kind of knowledge, say the transmission of cultural values. The contemporary Nigerian writer, though he cannot remain ignorant of scientific knowledge, explains the non-literate ways in ethnoscientific terms, which function, in their own contexts, as effectively as the methods of modern science.15 He also dons the bardic mantle of educating, both his own people as well as outsiders, in the truth about the African past. The two functions are really combined because the main truth that he wishes to convey is that the African world appears neither savage nor primitive in its own languages.

The continuity of oral into the written constitutes the major difference in the employment of orature in Nigerian fiction from that in Western literature. It is not only a symbolic device as in Western writing; it provides a metaphorical explanation of the world that is offered as a serious alternative to the rational empirical. Therefore, Africa's sophisticated orality does more than interrogate the primitivism myth; it encounters writing with other modes of perception. The novelists' preference for 'a mystical explanation' over the secular rational makes them one with the raconteurs of oral tales. We might recall that, in the secular rational prose of the bourgeois novel, these explanations did appear to be lacking in coherence. Remember Henderson's mock deferential tone in describing an African tribe that believes that the soul of the dead King is reincarnated in a lion's body.16 Or the profane gaze with which ancestor worship is cast in the popular romances of the Rider Haggard kind. The same themes, treated in a folk idiom, acquire a classical gravity that calls attention to the manner in which different 'languages' mediate experience. When one moves, say, from the travesties of Sacrifice in most Western literature on African, and its ritual significance in Soyinka's works, one realizes the near impossibility of describing one culture in the language of the other. If the rational secular language of the Western text cannot but profane mystical worlds, the African writer must resort to his native idiom to locate them in their own environments. As Achebe says,

Since Igbo people did not construct a rigid and closely argued system of thought to explain the universe and the place of man in it, preferring the metaphor of myth and poetry, anyone seeking an insight into their world must seek it along their own way. Some of these ways are folk-tales, proverbs, proper names, rituals and festivals.17

Let us examine Chinua Achebe's use of the folktale to illustrate how orature functions in Nigerian fiction.

II

Achebe's retellings of well-known African folktales in his novel have been examined from various perspectives. Bernth Lindfors' detailed discussion of the Kind and Unkind Girls in Arrow of God related it to Ezeulu's state of mind and explained it as a foreshadowing of Ezeulu's fate.18 Mary Ellen B Lewis, approving Achebe's excision of the tale in the interest of structural tightness, views the jealousy of the cowives in the tale as a reflection of Ugoye's way of sublimating her hostility.19 Barbara Harlow reads the Tortoise tale in Things Fall Apart as a paradigm for post-colonial resistance in the parrot's execution of revenge on the Tortoise by inverting Tortoise's message to his wife.20 Cathy Ramadan and

Donald Weinstock link the tale of the battle between the Earth and the Sky to the novel's thematic concern with masculine and feminine balance.21 Similarly, Traore reads the Mosquito and the Ear tale and of the Snake who ate up his mother as evidence of Okonkwo's gender imbalance. All these readings emphasize the symbolic function of the tales and justify their inclusion on structural or thematic grounds.22 Against these may be juxtaposed Emmanuel Obiechina's description of stories or "narrative proverbs" that locate them directly in the matrix of the African oral tradition. Though Obiechina agrees that "they function as images, metaphors and symbols, he contends that their embedding in the novels "produces a totally different narrative and epistemological situation." Linking the embedding of stories to the "two main principles of the African oral tradition -authority and association", he sees in "the tendency to validate individual positions by placing them within the objectifying matrices of stories and proverbs" as a way of marrying the oral with the written.23 Achebe's excision of his tale in Arrow of God as a 'structural weakness' is a compliance with the novel's unity requirement. The novel, as a rule, does not permit inclusion of unrelated material, which must, therefore, be provided a symbolic justification. On the other hand, oral narrative forms, such as the epic, abound with incidents and stories that have no direct bearing on the main action. While the folktales in Achebe's fiction might have thematic relevance as has been convincingly argued by several critics, they are governed by a poetic that disregards unity in the interest of fullness and variety for its own sake. Besides these tales, as the other genres

Achebe uses, are part of his strategy to represent Igbo culture through its own personalistic perspective rather than in the naturalistic categories of the Western ethnologist.24 The arrogance in the presumption of the native's incapability for self-representation except in the languages of the West can be met only through eschewing the Western episteme.

Achebe's resistance to Western ethnological discourse begins with the fundamental process of classification. In Things Fall Apart, he introduces us to Igbo folktale categories that do not conform to Western folklore types. In lumping together the Tortoise tale and that of the Quarrel between the Earth and the Sky as feminine tales Nwoye loved as opposed to the masculine tales of war and heroism, Achebe conflates fable and myth. It is not as if the Igbo do not distinguish between tales that have humans and those that have animals as characters but more attention is paid to the time, teller, occasion, audience and purpose of narration. It is these variables that separate Uchendu's telling of an animal tale in a serious parable from Ekwefi's story. In Nwoye's graduation from his mother's tales to the martial sagas retold by his father, we can detect a systematic learning scheme at work. If the feminine tales narrated traditionally by women highlight the mother's role in inculcating moral values in the young, the father's responsibility to educate the older children in the history and mores of the clan becomes evident in the manner Okonkwo takes over the instruction of the older boys. Nwoye's continuing preference for his mother's stories, on the other hand, underlines his adolescent anxieties about coming of age. As the clan elder Uchendu narrates the tale of Mother Kite to warn grown men, the folktale continues to provide the inputs for an adult learning programme. The etiological tale about how the Tortoise broke its Shell told by Ekwefi, the myth of the Earth and Sky quarrel, the fable of Mother Kite used by Uchendu as a parable, yield an understanding of the human and the natural. But to impose 'modern' terms in describing the wisdom in orality is to impose the methods of the modern onto the pre-modern and the literate on the non-literate. Folktales and myth are not the preliterate counterparts of Western science but alternative narratives of reality.

While it will be seen that Nigerian writer, too like the Western anthropologist, ends ups scribing his oral subject, orature is inducted primarily to eschew scriptocentric representation systems. The attempt to justify inclusion of folk items in the novel as structural links has its roots in the poetic that valorizes unity above all and is ignorant of narrative traditions sacrificing unity for delight in detail. Indian narratives, for instance, abound with material unconnected with the main conflict even in an oblique manner. Narration of known tales as part of an evening's entertainment is also not unknown in the Western epic.25 How is the first detailed folktale in the novel—about how the Tortoise broke its shell told by Ekwefi to be read? Is it thematically linked to the novel or does it exist as an interesting detail enjoyable for its own sake? Achebe's novel contains a large amount of anthropological details about Igbo customs and society rare in the novel but not uncommon in the epic. Just like the description of the proceedings of the native court by the egwugwu, the folktale fills in yet another dimension of traditional life. This movement—accretion rather than unity—is characteristic of oral narrative.26 If anything it brings out the strong role played by the mother in shaping the children's ethical values.

Achebe's Tortoise tale, a superb demonstration of the manner in which the storyteller individualizes a well known tale and locates it in its particular performance context, initiates the reader into the Igbo oral poetic against which he is invited to evaluate Achebe's translation of the Igbo world. The questions of originality and unity become redundant as Achebe introduces another version of the well-known folktale. Achebe\Ekwefi's virtuosity as a storyteller is evident when one compares it with other versions of the same tale.27 For one, Achebe is attentive to the performance contexts of the oral tale overlooked in most transcribed version. The tale is retold in response to a request to recreate the moonlit storytelling ambience. The delight in details, characteristic of oral narrative, fleshes out the known tale in the unique personality of the teller. Since it belongs to the category of tales told by women to children, it reflects the personality of the teller in its lingering on domestic details about the preparation of food, decoration of the house and details of household objects and the birds preening before the party. It follows the oral call-and-response dynamics in Ezinma's impatient interjection, "But the tortoise had no wings" at the outset and her complaint, on its conclusion, that it had no songs. Adapting its tone and language to its target audience comprising children, it reveals a sensitivity to its audience's knowledge and needs. The tale warns children against the evil consequence of greed, combining entertainment with education. The etiological ending, "This is how the Tortoise broke its shell" reinforces the folktale's status as an informal vehicle of instruction. If one accepts, as it is often suggested, that the poetics for African fiction must be derived from the novels themselves, this complete rendering of an African tale is the reader's guide to the way African narrative works. If Achebe aspires to reconnect with this tradition, his novel must follow the outline of the oral tale or epic. Obiechina highlights the role of the stories in defining the epistemological order within the novel." He explains how the story helps the novelist to construct a 'traditional' knowledge system based on analogy, allusion and metaphoric extension.28

Stories seem to be ubiquitous in the novel as in Igbo lives. There are stories to explain natural phenomena to children such as how leaves reduce in volume when cooked. But they also point out to grown adults the ways of the world or socially accepted behaviour. The other two tales in the novel—the Earth Sky Quarrel and the Mother Kite parable—similarly illustrate a non-literate culture's attempts to make sense of its world. While the first encapsulates the group's cosmology, the second is remarkable for its sharp observation of the animal world. Uchendu's attempt to solve a new problem through a traditional solution while highlighting the use of folktale precedents as a guideline to present action also records, as the solution fails to work, the inadequacy of the oral ways in resolving the problems ushered by literacy. Obiechina names this method of the African oral tradition—the use of the story to furnish illustrative, authoritative support to an idea, a point of view, a percept or perspective.29

The 'undifferentiated universe' of the folktale that personifies the non-human while permitting uninterrupted traffic between the human and the spirit best exemplifies the nature\ culture blurring in traditional thought that has baffled Western thinkers.30 Talking animals and birds are naturally more acceptable where the contiguity of the human and the non-human is taken for granted. While the non-human actors, who are merely human actors in masks, aid the folktale's gnomic function, they also point to a universe in which all nature is personalized. If we argue, as Levi-Strauss did, that the personalistic point of view translates abstractions into a concrete form, we are, in fact, perpetuating the anthropomorphism that the naturalistic point of view reduced this form of thinking to. The Earth Sky Quarrel is not a poetic explanation of scientific phenomena–the condition of drought–but a poetic mode of perception. When all nature is personalized, it is not difficult to view drought as a consequence of a humanized battle of will. It is important that we note that the traditional mind accepts these explanations literally. Not merely physical occurrences, but also metaphysical ideas are expressed in a personalized fashion as, for example, the concept of chi.

The tragic conflict in Achebe's novels cannot have its full impact unless understood in the light of this central concept of Igbo cosmology that Achebe attempted to explain in an essay in Morning Yet on Creation Day.31 Though several references are made to the folktale about the wrestler who challenged his chi in connection with Okonkwo in Things Fall Apart, the folktale is used by Ezeulu in Arrow of God in his address to the people of

Umuaro. Ruth Finnegan informs us that folktales were often used to illustrate important points in oratory as Ezeulu does here.32 Ezeulu cites it to admonish his clan for carrying a message of war to their neighbours in Okperi disregarding his advice. Ironically, the same tale is used to condemn Ezeulu's recalcitrance when he refuses to eat the Sacred Yam in accordance with his clan's wishes. And Achebe, trying to explain the Igbo concept, like his Igbo people, resorts to the "metaphor of myth and poetry" by citing the same tale in his essay. Achebe's use of the parabolic mode in elucidating a complex metaphysical idea corroborates the thesis about the status of folk stories as embodiments of Igbo thought. As has been pointed out earlier, the folktale is not fictionalization or a metaphorical representation of an abstract concept. For the Igbo cosmos demarcated by Achebe into the land of the living and that of the spirits in his essay is also visualized as a concrete spatial zone. The cautionary tale about setting limits to human aspiration expresses it as a wrestling match ending in the defeat of the human by the spirit. The Igbo belief in a spirit being complementing the human being in the spirit world and presiding over his creation as well as the allotment of his destiny and character is interpreted quite literally.33 Just as the wrestler crossing over into the land of the spirits does not invite disbelief in Ezeulu's audience, his viewing Umuaro's cry of battle against Okperi as a challenge to Ulu does not strike them as improbable. As in the folktale, humans may journey into spirit worlds in Achebe's fiction. Like the embedded tales, the novels, too, personify the non-human and dissolve the distinction between the natural and cultural. The transition from

Ekwefi's tale to the mysterious summons to Ezinma from Agbala is equally smooth because both the tale and the novel inhabit the same universe.

Traditional histories' notion of divine motivation, as in Ezeulu's warning and in Umuaro's seeing the hand of Ekwensu in Akukalia's death, conflicts with the manner of Western histories as underlined by the Umuaro legend. The two versions of the creation myth of Umuaro, recounted by Ezeulu and Nwaka in their respective speeches, illustrate not only the folktale as a source of historical knowledge but also the difference in a memory-based historiography.34 The authority of the father in a system that transmits knowledge of the past from father to son does not rule out the availability of several versions of the same text. In the absence of a unified text, which version is more correct? Ezeulu cites the authority of his father to put forward his argument that Umuaro was given a piece of land to live in by Okperi along with their deities. Nwaka rebuts this through a different story he had from his father, which has Okperi people as wanderers. This understanding, 'knowledge of the land' as relative as it is retained in individual memory conflicts with the permanence of written historiography. Since this 'lore of the land' carries the same authority as any written document in the settlement of the present territorial dispute how are the various versions to be reconciled? Nwaka's contradictory statement that the 'lore of the land is beyond the knowledge of many fathers' (335) fits in with Igbo division of their past.35 Nwaka is successful in exploiting the contradictory versions of the Umuaro legend to his advantage, as the 'living' versions do not resolve in one consensual version.36 Through Akukalia and his companion's conversation we gather that before the coming of the white man the two villages had not bothered about the ownership of the land letting present practice determine how it was shared. Akukalia 'remembers' coming with his father to cut grass from the piece of land being claimed by Okperi now, which his companions believes is due to the white man's reminder. The British offer many instances of imposing on these memory-based methods their own system of private property and written documentation in mapping colonial spaces.

Though the revised version of Arrow of God cuts short the long tale, the novel remains in the legend mode. There is, for instance, the Idemili legend narrated by his priest to Nwaka as an etiological tale about the custom of hanging the heads of Ezeulu and Ezedemili at death. Ezedimili links this custom to Ulu's recent birth as opposed to Ezedimili's antiquity to trace the present enmity between the two priests to the arrogance of Ulu's Chief Priest. But the new convert Moses Unachukwu's plea to the new missionary for not killing the royal Python by narrating the tale of the six brothers who killed the python reveals the continuation of the oral modes of perception despite the arrival of new religion and literacy. Moses' animism -the royal Python as kinsmen- does not conflict with his belief in the Christian Scriptures. Oduche, the first to be inducted in the zone of literacy, still remembers this tale from his childhood even though he may cite scriptural passages against the serpent. And his residual fear of the Python's curse prevents him from actually killing it when he sets out to do so. When Ugoye narrates the folktale about the two wives to the rest of the children, Oduche is seen to be holding his new book Azu Ndu from which he painfully tries to form the first few words. As the two modes of instruction are juxtaposed, folktale against the primer, we become aware not only of the poverty of writing in Oduche's halting words but also his gradual alienation from the oral shared by the rest of Ezeulu's children. This mode spills over from the folktale into the novel as the farm at the boundary of the land of men and the land of the spirits finds a parallel in Ezeulu's half man half spirit nature.

The shift from an oral conceptuality to that created by literacy is signaled through the displacement of folktale by the Western literary text in No Longer at Ease.37 Among the heathen items that Nwoye\Isaac bans from his household is folktales that his wife would prefer telling to her children than reading the Bible. Isaac's fetishization of writing is matched with the contemporary prestige of white man's knowledge captured in the folk idiom as 'knowing book'. Obi's 'knowing book' is in direct proportion to his ignorance of tales from the Igbo repertoire. The schoolboy, who is nicknamed Dictionary for his fluency in alien English, is publicly shamed when he cannot narrate a folktale in the Oral class until his mother secretly comes to his rescue. Though Obi displays an obvious relish in these stories in the manner he improvises on the Leopardess tale, his allusions become increasingly literary. From the callow nostalgic poem he composes, to his frequent references to Eliot, Greene, Conrad and other canonical Western works, his conversion to the modes of literacy is inversely related to his distancing from Igbo oral modes, such as his failure to interpret the Igbo song about the in-law during his ride to his village, or his code switching to English in a speech to the Umuofia Union he began in Igbo. This code switching reflects Obi's perceptual shift from Igbo modes of conceptualization. He is repeatedly reminded that 'knowing book', that is, being literate in the white man's language and ways, has nothing to do with being wise as defined in Igbo terms. The folktale about the Tortoise who refuses to attend his mother's funeral that Obi overhears brings home to Obi the distance he has traveled from the folkland by knowing book. The displacement of oral modes with those of literacy is recorded through the ineffectiveness of the folktale as a parabolic device in altered circumstances.

The universe of Anthills of the Savannah is far removed both from the village world of the novels set in the precolonial past and the postindependence setting of the urban novels.38 Even though Obi Okonkwo and Odili Samalu have moved away from the pristine precolonial orality to the corrupt postcolonial present, they are essentially first generation literates still umbilically attached to their native milieu. The troika ruling Anthills, friends from their schooldays in Lord Lugards, are, on the other hand, the true African elites steeped thoroughly in Western mores. Most characters in this novel share Beatrice's exposure to all traditional other than their own that Achebe the storyteller does not. As in his previous novels he positions the Igbo myth about the abuse of power at the heart of the novel. Though Beatrice and others might remain oblivious to the significance of the Idemili myth, the reader is invited to view Nigerian military's abuse of power in the light of traditional Igbo checks on the exercise of individual authority. The one who aspires to the highest title in traditional Igbo society is required to perform so many ceremonies that drain him financially. A related issue is the unknown divine factor in deciding the worthiness of the aspirant to a high title. As in the story about the randy title seeker, power in traditional societies was bestowed with a number of taboos and responsibilities. The myth is Achebe's means of guiding his reader into the traditional Igbo code. Unlike the Igbo title seeker, Sam not only does not deem it fit to solicit divine sanction but also ignores Idemili's warning like the man in the story. Nor does he recognize, unlike his Igbo predecessor, that no man can take the high and sacred title without the approval and support of Idemili.

Though the wisdom in folktales is not able to meet the problems created by literacy, the novels do not deny it the status of wisdom. Even in Anthills of the Savannah, Achebe gives the final word to the Abazon elder the bastion of a dying wisdom. In the sleazy precincts of the Harmony Hotel, the old man transports the archaic dignity of Arrow of God. Through the village elder, Achebe recasts the history of contemporary Nigeria in the language of preliterate legend.

It is the story, not the others, that saves our progeny from blundering like blind beggars into the spikes of the cactus force. The story is our escort, without it, we are blind. Does the blind man own his escort? No, neither do us the story, rather it is the story that owns us and directs us.

Chapter 3

Oral Dynamics of Things Fall Apart

'D. Bamidele

CHARLES Bodunde had cited Joel Adedeji on the function of "the complex corpus of verbal or spoken art" in oral literature as "a means of recalling the past based on ideas, beliefs, symbols, assumptions, attitudes and sentiments of peoples" (1). And Ajadi, following Bukenya and Nandwa in Isidore Okpewho who describe Oral literature "as those utterances, whether spoken, recited or sung, whose composition and performances exhibit to an appreciable degree the artistic characteristics of accurate observation, vivid imagination and ingenious expression" (238), opines that we need to internalize the fact that African oral literature embraces the entire spectrum of the African way of life, thoughts and ideas in terms of the philosophy, feelings, behaviours, psychology, the African relationship in terms of socio-cultural values, etc. For Na'Allah:

Traditional Africa was a basically oral society. Our history, science, medicine, technology, philosophy and literary forms were passed through the words of mouth in myths, folktales, legends, proverbs, praise poetry and ritual performances. It is the main mode of Africa's religious worship. It is the important mode of education and communication in the continent. It is the main mode of transmitting knowledge and keeping records. Above all, oral literature is the embodiment of African values and aspirations. (102)

Bodunde argues that the "aggregational values of African worldview form a vast continuum of functional aesthetic values" (61). In his words, "Myths, legends, archetypal patterns, heroic traditions, folktales, proverbs, riddles, topical and political songs, apart from influencing the formal literature, provide effective revolutionary aesthetics for explaining the dynamics of history and growth" (61). Critics have noted that "traditional African culture is oral, and (that) the literature in the forms of epic, legend, folktale, song and others is transmitted by words of mouth from one generation to another" (Ojaide 44). Bodunde adapts Joel Adedeji's ideas to provide a typology of this oral tradition, which recognizes the literary and historical (1). The literary category includes poetic forms like Oriki praise and totem chants, Odu or Ifa divination poems and songs of the Yoruba in South West Nigeria. Included in this category are other forms like incantations, parables and proverbs. The historical type includes such forms of narratives based on myths, legends and historical genres like sagas and epics. Kofi Awonoor's typology is broader than Adedeji's. He identifies three broad categories of drama, prose narrative and poetry. For drama, he includes types like masquerades, festivals, ritual performances and ceremonies pertaining to the secret societies. For prose genre, he accepts William Bascom's 'three pronged' division of folktale, myth and legend. Poetry genre includes forms like praise poetry, religious poetry, incantations, lullaby and occupational poetry (69). Chinweizu et al's functional-aesthetic approach in providing a link between orality and what Walter J. Ong calls the technologization of the word (written culture) is relevant here:

Orature is the incontestable reservoir of the values, sensibilities, aesthetics and achievements of traditional African thought and imagination outside the plastic arts. Thus, it must serve as the ultimate foundation, guidepost, and point of departure for a modern liberated African Literature. It is the root from which modern African Literature must draw sustenance. (2)

Oral Dynamics of the Written Text

The issue of "aesthetic transfer" has been a subject of critical controversies whereby critics have, over the years, argued on the possibility of Black Aesthetics rooted in African ways and mannerisms. It is thus possible to identify Igbo traditional values and Yoruba cultural ideologues in Achebe and Soyinka, respectively. Because of the roots of orature in authentic written African literature, this domestication or Africanization helps it wear the garb of the total African existential experience, even though it is written in a foreign language.

Afrocentric critics have, therefore, argued that whoever wants to make a reasonable and responsible criticism of African literature must be rooted in African culture and general belief systems. This is primarily accounted for by the reason that modern African writers bring to their work cultural histories and linguistic styles unknown to English until recently. Little wonder why an American scholar admits that "despite the proliferation of 'experts', whites are unable to evaluate the Black Experience, and consequently, any work of art derived from it or addressed to those who live it" (Lindfors 1). Bernth Lindfors had cited Achebe's complaint of "getting a little weary of all the special types of criticism which have been designed for us by people whose knowledge of us is very limited" (2). Although he had argued that any race that claim a monopoly on critical sensitivity is advocating "aesthetic apartheid", as against Ernest Emenyonu's avowal that "what many Western critics issue on African literature is a reflection of a profound lack of knowledge about African cultural traditions coupled with an ignorance of the existence, nature and depth of the heritage of African oral literature" (3), Lindfors nevertheless admits that "bearers of a culture are better equipped to interpret that culture than aliens who have experienced its realities only vicariously" (2).

The above is to emphasize the fact that modern African literature is an admixture of traditional oral art and technologized, written tradition. Bodunde justifies the rationale for heavy leaning of the modern written art on the traditional verbal art. "Current aesthetic practices among black artists", he notes, "indicate a growing interest in the techniques of the oral artists who situate their art in the African social and cosmic setting" (2). For Mazisi Kunene, "these kinds of settings are indeed the primary basis of all literatures" (2) and mark the writer's recognition of the great importance of verbal art in society. William Bascom, A. H.Gayton and O. F. Raum provide a raison d'etre for this heavy traffic. They offer that myths and legends do not only contain detailed descriptions of the religious system of the people but also function as the educational system and instruments of both self-control and for the control of others. Decolonizing African literature is therefore consequential to the belief that orature is a literary Mecca from where African writers draw inspiration in showcasing their rich cultural heritage rather than following dogmas of some alien, aesthetic standards. This ongoing tradition of 're-inventing' the traditional modes of aesthetic expression in the written medium is a way of responding to the challenges of an evolving black aesthetics.

In setting the criteria for examining a text's relation with oral traditions, three tests have been prescribed by Richard Dorson thus: "Biographical evidence that the author has enjoyed direct contact with oral lore, internal evidence indicating the author's familiarity with folklore; corroborative evidence 'that the saying, tale, song, or custom inside the literary work possesses an independent traditional life" (qtd. in Bodunde 3-4) There seems enough reason for African art to wear cultural outfits since an individual is sometimes defined by the cultural personality he wears. This attachment to cultural landscape is inevitable in African literature since it is part of the molding block that builds the artist's educational, social, religions and cosmic consciousness. Thus the truly original writer, borrowing from Lindfors, is the one endowed with a "historical sense ... a perspective not

55

only of the pastness of the past, but of its presence. He must be conscious of the living heritage of his culture and at the same time, aware of his own place in it and relationship to it" (24).

Oral Dynamics of Things Fall Apart

It was earlier stated that African novelists draw their inspiration from oral tradition. Thus "modern African interaction is a sibling of traditional African oral literature", and "since African oral literature is a museum of the totality of African heritage ... it is therefore, a valid pursuit for modern African creative writers to visit it and eke out their artistic raw materials (Bamidele 10).

Chinua Achebe is one of such modern African writers who navigate the ancient waters of African orature in his creative enterprise. Achebe in his novels makes use of oral traditions in a manner that justifies the observation that "for many modern African writers, the oral literature can be a source of strength" (qtd in Ohaeto 1). In fact, Achebe's narrative grammar in Things Fall Apart is reminiscent of the narrator of folktales under the moonlight in a traditional context. Achebe utilizes these oral features to suit his fictive purpose as he demonstrates in the conscious use of metaphor and idiomatic expressions, proverbial lore and folktales to drive home his message emphatically. Even the title, Things Fall Apart, taken from a poem entitled The Second Coming by W.B. Yeats, assumes a metaphor for the confusion and disharmony unleashed on a clan which "once thought like one, shared a common awareness and acted like one" (v) by the white man's education and religion. But beyond Yeats, this traditional consciousness of Things Fall Apart is best captured through the words of Obierika: "Now he has won our brothers and our clan can no longer act like one. He has put a knife on the things that held us together and we have fallen apart" (v).

The magnitude of aesthetic transfer in Achebe's Things Fall Apart becomes even more poignant when the language of the novel is considered. The proverbs, idiomatic expressions and similes are drawn from the author's cultural landscape, and one can, at once, feel and see the curves and contours of the Igbo cultural map. It has been observed of Achebe's fiction that the "proverbs serve as keys to an understanding of his novels because he uses them not merely to add local colour but to sound and reiterate themes, to sharpen characterization, to clarify, and to focus on the values of the society he is portraying" (Ohaeto, 19). Early in the novel, Achebe himself states that "among the Igbo, the art of conversation is regarded very highly, and proverbs are the palm oil with which words are eaten" (ix). This generous use of oral materials can be explained in terms of the fact that the author himself is part of Igbo cultural essence, and this tremendously manifests in his creative enterprise. Aigboje Higo, in the preliminary comments to the novel says Achebe's "is the skill acquired by good story tellers" (ix). For instance the story teller is abstruse about Unoka's apparent laziness. Unoka, Okonkwo's father tells Okoye his creditor that "the sun will shine on those who stand before it shines on those who kneel under them" (6) as a way of appealing for patience since even the man he owes a thousand cowries had not come to wake him up in the morning for it. But we can note his endearing attitude to the hero who somewhat represents the strength and weakness of the land. Achebe describes Okonkwo in terms of his towering personal achievements at a very tender age; he is already one of the greatest men of his time in the very presence of elders because "as the elders said, if a child washed his hands he could eat with kings" (60).

In a traditional setting moon lit nights are full of activities; children play in open fields and adults play in not so open places, and even the old remember their youth, thus, "when the moon is shining, the cripple becomes hungry for a walk" (7). Nwakibie's prayer for peaceful co-existence among the people of the clan and curse for the harbinger of trouble is couched thus: "Let the kite perch and let the eagle perch too. If one says no to the other, let his wing break" (14). Okonkwo appreciates that respect is reciprocal and he offers that, "a man who pays respect to the great paves way for his own greatness" (14). He pays due respect to his benefactor, Nwakibie, before requesting for his seed yams. Ogbuefi Idigo describes Obiako's sudden departure from his palm wine tapping trade due to a warning from the oracle that he would fall off a palm tree and kill himself in an alluring proverb, "A toad does not run in the daytime for nothing" (15).

The mere mention of Obiako's late father's inability to own a fowl before he died reminds Okonkwo of his father's financial weakness: "an old woman is always uneasy when dry bones are mentioned in a proverb" (15). In the days when young men are afraid of hard work, Okonkwo praises himself for clearing a farm even though he has no yams to plant. Thus "the lizard that jumped from the high Iroko tree to the ground said he would praise himself if no one else did" (16). Nwakibie likens his precautionary measure of not giving out his yam seeds to lazy men who would simply bury them in heaps and abandon them to "Eneke the bird who says that since men have learnt to shoot without missing, he has learnt to fly without perching" (16) and in ascribing to Okonkwo's worthiness of his yam seeds he says, "you can tell a ripe corn by its look" (16). Achebe in describing Okonkwo's sudden rise from poverty and misfortune to great wealth and opulence says, "looking at a king's mouth, one would think he never sucked at his mother's breast" (19). Okonkwo's haughtiness and brusqueness in treating less successful men is castigated in the following proverb: "those whose Palm kernels were cracked for them by a benevolent spirit should not forget to be humble" (19). But Achebe negates the above claim by referencing Okonkwo's grim struggle against poverty and misfortune and concludes that "when a man says yes his chi says yes also. Okonkwo said yes very strongly, so his chi agreed" (19). In expressing his fear of Nwoye being a weakling and unfit to take his position after he leaves, Okonkwo says "a chick that will grow into a cock can be spotted the very day it hatches" (46). When Obierika bemoans Okonkwo's involvement in the killing of Ikemefuna, the latter defends himself thus: "a child's fingers are not scalded by a piece of hot yam which its mother puts into its palm" (47) since it was the oracle that decreed that Ikemefuna be killed. Maduka, Obierika's son's smartness is likened to his father's when he was young because "when mother-cow is chewing grass, its young ones watch its mouth" (49). When Okonkwo inadvertently kills Ezeudu's son and is banished from Umuofia to Mbanta, Obierika, his friend, laments his friend's misfortune for an offence he committed unwittingly but the decision to banish him is justified thus: "If one finger brought oil, it soiled the others" (87).

Achebe also makes use of metaphors and similes to paint vivid pictures of the events and situations at hand. During the wrestling match between Amalinze the cat and Okonkwo, Achebe describes the former as "a wily craft man" and the latter as "slippery as a fish in water" (3). Okonkwo's struggle with poverty saw him engage in share cropping which only yields a third of the harvest, and from this he supports his mother and two sisters; his effort is likened to "pouring grains of corn into a bag full of holes" (16). "The earth burned like hot coals and wasted all the yams that had been sown" (17) when the rains came late and blazing sun became fierce to Umuofians and "that year the harvest was sad, like a funeral" (17).

Okonkwo is chosen by the nine villages to carry a message of war to their enemies or atone for the murder of Udo's wife but the enemies "retreated and treated Okonkwo like a king and brought him a virgin who was given to Udo as wife, and the lad Ikemefuna" (20). When Okonkwo broke the week of peace, his enemies call him "the little bird nza who so far forgot himself after a heavy meal that he challenged his chi" (22) for his good fortune had gone into his head. A corn-cob with only a few scattered grains is likened to "eze agadi wayi" or the teeth of an old woman" (25). In describing the effect of drumming on the people, Achebe says, "the air shivered and grew tense like a tightened bow" (35). Ikemefuna's rapid growth is described as "rapidly like a yam tendril in the rainy season ..." (37). The arrival of locusts is shown as "tiny eyes of light like shinning star-dust" (39). After Okonkwo kills Ikemefuna, he suffers insomnia and loss of appetite and "felt like a drunken giant walking with the limbs of a mosquito" (44). Okonkwo exaggerates Nwoye's weakness thus: "A bowl of pounded yam can throw him in a wrestling match" (46). Obierika lampoons the traditional custom that forbids titled men from climbing tall palm trees but can tap short ones. He says the custom "is like Dimaragana, who would not lend his knife for cutting up dog-meat because dog meat was a taboo to him, but offered to use his teeth" (48). And "as sharp as razor" (49) is used to describe Maduka's swiftness in movement. The cordial and friendly atmosphere with which Akueke's bride price is being handled is described as "if I fall down for you and you fall down for me, it is play" (51) while in Abame and Aninta bride-price is haggled and bargained "as if they were buying a goat or cow in the market" (51). Amadi's leprosy is euphemistically the "the white skin" (52). "Okonkwo stood by, rumbling like thunder in the rainy season" (58) is a literary description of his tangential flights in moments of uncontrollable anger and temper.

A moonless evening in Umuofia is "as black as charcoal" (67) and exaggerated with "one could not have known where one's mouth was in the darkness ..." (67). "His body rattled like a piece of dry stick in his empty shell" (68) is used to describe the effect of famine on Tortoise. Chielo's voice in trance is described as "cracking like the angry bark of thunder ..." (71) and Ekwefi's aloofness when Chielo takes her only daughter away is "like a hen whose only chick has been carried away by a kite" (72). "The Hills and the Caves were as silent as death" (78) while "Obierika's compound was as busy as an ant hill" (78). The market of Umuike is so full and busy that "if you threw up a grain of sand it would not find a way to fall to earth again" and "they can steal your cloth from off your waist in that market" (79).

Songs are also important elements of oral traditions. They make the stories vivid, heighten the intensity of the narrative and create a rapport in most cases between the story-teller and the reader. In Things Fall Apart, Achebe employs songs to reinforce the themes, capture the mood of the novel and provide critical perspectives on the activities and interactions of the characters. The first song in the novel is sung by children to herald the recession of the once heavy rains: "The rain is falling, the sun is shining, alone Nnadi is cooking and eating" (25).

Okafo's victory in the wrestling match at the Ilo is celebrated by his supporters who sang his praise while young women clapped their hands:

Who will wrestle for our village?
Okafo will wrestle for our village.
Has he thrown a hundred men?
He has thrown four hundred men.
Has he thrown a hundred cats?
He has thrown four hundred cats.
Then send him word to fight for us. (36)

As Ikemefuna is being led to the forest where he will be killed, he suddenly remembers his mother and the thought also came to his mind that she might be dead. He sings a game-song that will determine his mother's condition, but ironically he never gets to find out:

Eze elina, elina!
Sala
Eze ilikwa ya
Ikwaba akwa oligholi
Ebe Dauda nechi eze
Ebe Uzulu nete egwu
Sala. (42)

The song at the end of Obierika's daughter's wedding sets the tone and mood of the occasion and the characters:

If I hold her hand
She says, "Don't touch!"
If I hold her foot
She says, "Don't touch!"
But when I hold her waist beads,
She pretends not to know! (83)

Kotma, foreigners from Umuru, serve the white man as court messengers. They are hated by Umuofians for their arrogance and high-handedness to their fellow brothers. Umuofians lampoon them with the following song:

Kotma of the ash buttocks,
He is fit to be a slave
The white man has no sense,
He is fit to be a slave. (123)

Achebe also utilizes folktales in weaving beautiful patterns in his fictive enterprise. He does not make direct evaluative statements about his literary personae. To understand his works fully, therefore, one has to understand his use of tales (Umeasiegbu 2). Achebe uses his tales to pass moral judgments on his characters, especially the erring ones. In Things Fall Apart (38), Achebe narrates the story of the vulture that is sent to the sky to ask for rain. There is a feud between Earth and Sky so the latter withholds rain for seven years. Crops are scotched to death; there is famine and even the dead cannot be buried. Vulture is mandated to take man's supplication to the Sky to release rain. Sky grants Vulture's request. He wraps rain in cocoyam leaves and gives to vulture. Vulture sets out for home but on his way, he pierces the cocoyam leaves in which rain is wrapped and rain fell as it had never fallen before. Vulture could not return home to deliver his message but flew to a distant land where he saw a fire. Vulture gets to the fire and finds out that it was a man making a sacrifice; he warmed himself in the fire and ate the entrails (38).

This tale might have captured Okonkwo's sudden rise to become one of the most important men in his time and while he thinks he is making progress, he, like the vulture, drops from grace to grass due to his inability to be analytical in his judgments. He is ruled by impulses. It is possible that this tale is a sign of Achebe's negative judgment on Okonkwo his protagonist. He likens him to the vulture, an irresponsible and despicable bird. There is also the tale of the tortoise in Things Fall Apart (67-70) that is strictly for moral evaluation. Once, all animals were invited to a feast in the sky. The location of the venue implies that only winged animals can attend. Tortoise intends to go even though he has no wings, he seeks help from some birds but they are reluctant to assist him because he is unreliable. He promises to change his attitude and, on this note, the birds lend him some feathers. They had hardly got to the sky when tortoise started his usual trickery, consequent upon which his companions had nothing to eat. In order to get even with him, they took their feathers back from the ingrate so that he will be stranded in the sky. He fell from the sky to earth and broke his shell.

Like Tortoise, Okonkwo's sudden rise in Umuofia is as a result of the assistance he receives from people, for instance, it is Nwakibie who gives him the first yam seeds. Just as tortoise's downfall is as a result of excessive exploitation of his benefactor's assistance, so also is Okonkwo's fall a result of his trampling upon the customs of the clan, and disregarding the counsel of friends like Ezeudu and Obierika. Okonkwo's downfall climaxes when he hangs himself. Once again, Achebe castigates Okonkwo's moral weakness by likening him to the tortoise, which is known for its archetypal cunning, disloyalty, treachery, indecision, self-deceit and arrogance (Umeasiegbu, 4).

Praises are an important form of orature. Evil Forest, the leader of the masquerades that make up the clan praises himself thus: "I am the dry meat that fills the mouth, I am the fire that burns without faggots" (66), and a cow is referred to as "The one that uses its tail to drive flies away" (80). Curses are also rampant in the novel:

"whether you are a spirit or man, may Agbala shave your head with a blunt razor! May he twist your neck until you see your heels!" (73). Chielo, the priestess of Agbala greets her god thus: "the owner of the future, the messenger of earth, the god who cut man down when his life was sweetest to him" (75).

Okonkwo's dislike for Nwoye's incipient laziness and inability to prepare yam seeds earns him a reprimand: "Amadioha will break your head for you!" (24). The dramatization of festivals like the new yam festival (26), burial rites (84-85), and offering of sacrifices to gods (25) are in consonance with the fact that man exploits the animate and inanimate objects below him to expiate his gods. This is in accordance with J.S. Mbiti's description of the pyramidal structure of the African universe. The performance of Egwugwu as dramatized in the novel (63-64) is not only for entertainment but also for moral evaluation as they are seen settling disputes between warring members of the clan. Uchendu's speech (93-95) and Egonwanne whose sweet tongue can change fire into cold ash (141) are highly oratorical. Achebe's appreciation of what he calls Igbo oratory and his effort to preserve it is seen in his near obsession with the exploration of it in his own novels, particularly Things Fall Apart and Arrow of God (Egejuru 394). Things Fall Apart is replete with numerous Igbo words without translation and the narrative is densely populated with the description of Igbo custom and culture. Like Charlie Sugnet, it is easy to see "the truth of Igbo society from the inside. … without being asked to judge, … and how the destruction of any element of their world-view threatened the whole fabric of coherence in which they lived" (85).

Myths also feature prominently in Things Fall Apart. The locust myth (37-40) is a metaphor for the invasion of Abame, and Mbanta and Umuofia by the new dispensation. The epic rise of Okonkwo and his triumph over the unbeatable Amalinze the Cat (3) makes him a founding ancestor and thus constitutes the foundation myth of Umuofia. The Mosquito and Ear story (53) symbolizes the gender conflict that perpetually pitches Okonkwo against the female principles. Okonkwo wants to be seen always as a strong man, so he is constantly at war with the weak man syndrome. His constant fear of being considered weak leads him tragically to his end.

This discourse is best concluded on Achebe's pronouncement on the parameters of the thought that govern Things Fall Apart thus:

Since the Igbo people did not construct a rigid and closely argued system of thought to explain the universe and the place of man in it, preferring the metaphor of myth and poetry, anyone seeking an insight into their world must seek it along their own way. Some of these ways are folktales, proverbs, proper names, rituals and festivals. (qtd in Traore 342)

It is obvious that a reader who is alien to the cultural geography of Achebe's Igbo ideologue would need further tutelage in African oral traditions to get to the core of meanings even though it is written in English. Oral traditions continue to play important roles in the literary enterprise of authentic African writers. Achebe's engagement with oral tradition has placed an authentic African stamp on his art.

Chapter 4

Orality in the Works of Ousmane Sembène

J W Bouchard

THE majority of Ousmane Sembène's literary and cinematic work is a critique of the conflictual relationships between the colonizer and the colonized, the state and the people, the rich and the poor, and the elders and the youth. Thus, his novels and films address issues involving tensions that are commonly created by uneven power relations. Well-known novels by Sembène include Les bouts de bois de dieu (1960), L'Harmattan (1964), and Xala (1974). In 1963, he created his first short film "Borom Saret" (1963), followed one year later by "Niaye" (1964). In 1966, Sembène completed "La Noire de ...", his first full-length film that won first prize at the Film Festival of Carthage and gained him the title of Best African Filmmaker at the World Festival of Negro Arts in Dakar. Films to follow included "Le Mandat" (1968), "Emitai" (1971), "Xala" (1974), "Ceddo" (1977), "Camp de Thiaroye" (1988), "Guelewar" (1992), "Faat Kiné" (2000) and "Molaadé" (2004). Though one could write numerous articles on the themes covered by Sembène's large, multimedia corpus (poverty, African feminisms, circumcision, religion, politics, etc.), one aspect of profound interest is the role of the griot, or West African storyteller, in Sembène's work.

Before the written word became a prevalent form of self-expression in West Africa, the griot served as the oral historian, musician, and entertainer of the community. His role was complex, and became even more so during and after French colonial rule. The modern griot's function shifted along with the extreme sociopolitical change Senegal experienced during its emergence as a nation after independence. As West African countries, such as Senegal, sought to establish a national identity, the griot's role became increasingly political. During this time, many self-proclaimed griots and artists emerged. Ousmane Sembène was one of the most prolific and influential members of this group of professional modern day griots.

This study will examine the role of the griot in Sembène's literary and film work and how his portrayal of this character becomes a self-reflexive commentary on his own role as an artist in contemporary society. Of course, language plays an essential role in Sembène's griotic project. By using both French and Wolof in his work, Sembène plays with formations of la francophonie as both a linguistic and cultural construction. Can one be defined as a francophone artist if he still uses Wolof in his work? Where does "l'africanisme" end and la francophonie begin? Thus Sembène's self-proclaimed position as griot becomes increasingly hybridized as he chooses to employ two distinct languages in his projects. Furthermore, this inherently hybrid stance opens up a new realm of "francophone" literary and cinematic production.

The term griot carries myriad cultural connotations. Traditionally, West African griots belonged to a certain caste. Within the Senegalese griot the caste, there existed a series of subgroups, including the géwel, jéli and géer. Moreover, the griot tradition had a hereditary component in that only descendants of a certain lineage had the ability to become griots and access to the knowledge and skills of former griots. The European term, griot, is a derivation of a Portuguese word meaning, "to cry or to call." However, the term griot has been appropriated by and is most frequently associated with the French language; the terms griot and griotte are employed to describe male and female storytellers, respectively.

The function of a griot is a complex mixture of storytelling, historical preservation, and performance. The traditional role of the griot was historically and continues to be controversial. He belonged to the lowest cast, yet, by virtue of his societal function, he was privy to much historical and political information. In fact, one of his assigned tasks was to preserve the history of the country through story and song. In his book entitled Le Maître de la parole, the Guinean author Camara Laye states:

En vértié, le griot (…) avant d'être historien, est, avant tout, un artiste et en corollaire, ses chants, ses epopées et ses légendes, des oeuvres d'art. La tradition orale tient donc de l'art plus que de la science. Et tout comme le sculpteur africain, la réalité historique placée devant le

71

griot n'est pas contée par telle qu'elle apparait. (Laye, 21).

In truth, the griot (…), before being a historian, is, above all, an artist. Therefore, it would follow that his songs, chants, poems and legends are all works of art. The oral tradition is more closely related to art than to science. Exactly like the African sculptor, the historical reality placed in front of the griot is not always told as it is. (Author's translation)

This quote describes the "artistic" license taken by griots when recounting historic narratives in society. During the colonial period, this "artistic license" became even more subjective and problematic. Since storytelling was how the griot made his living, his stories often changed according to the social or political agenda of his patron. One can hardly criticize the griot for ensuring his financial survival, however, this aspect of the griot's existence calls in to question the authenticity of his historical accounts. The role of the griot is commonly compared to that of the Renaissance artist forced, by virtue of his social standing and profession, to seek patronage from wealthy noblemen in order to pursue his own artistic projects. However, at a certain point, his projects no longer become his, and he is used purely as a political tool for those in power.

Through his work as a cinematographer and writer, Sembène calls for a re-interpretation of the griot's role in contemporary Africa. Sembène's claim to being a "new griot" is essentially political, beyond its obvious articulation of artistic camaraderie . with other contemporary genres, including film, literature, visual arts, and music. By relating the author or cinematographer to the West African griot, he calls for a re-interpretation of past griotic functions. In doing so, he both critiques and redefines the role of the griot in West African society.

In order to fully understand how Sembène views his role, it is necessary to explore his personal relationship to the term "griot". He is not a géwel by birth (that is to say, he does not belong to the traditional griot caste), but he is a griot by trade. This professional association gives him the liberty to redefine and re-explore to the role of the griot in contemporary society. In addition, the title of "griot" serves to authenticate his body of literary and film work among the African artistic intelligentsia. As David Murphy states in his book Sembène: Imagining Alternatives in Film and Fiction:

The modern African writer is often compared to the traditional griot, with the purpose of such a comparison usually being to link the contemporary African writer to a traditional form of African storytelling. As a result, the author's work is given the stamp of that most problematic of concepts, 'authenticity.' (Murphy 54).

In addition to defining himself as a griot as a means of lending authenticity to his corpus, Sembène is primarily concerned with redefining the griot as a character who upholds truth and justice in the face of moral corruption. In his own work, Sembène vows to remain close to the experience of the people. The following citation, found in the avertissement de l'auteur, (Author's Note) at the beginning of Sembène's novel, L'Harmattan, describes his artistic vision as he associates the role of the modern novelist with that of the traditional storyteller.

Je ne fais pas la théorie du romain africain. Je me souviens pourtant que jadis, dans cette Afrique qui passe pour classique, le griot était non seulement l'élément dynamique de sa tribu, clan, village, mais aussi le témoin patent de chaque événement. C'est lui qui enregsitrait, déposait devant tous, sous l'arbre du palabre, les faits et gestes de chacun. La conception de mon travail découle de cet enseignement: rester au plus près du réel et du peuple. (Sembène, L'Harmattan, 3).

I don't theorize about the African novel. However, I remember that in the so-called classical Africa of the past, the griot was not only the dynamic figure in the tribe, clan, or village, but also the chief witness to every major event. It was he who recorded and who, under the palaver tree, recited the events and acts of everyone before the entire community. My conception of my work flows from this teaching: one must remain as close as possible to reality and to the people. (Author's translation)

This passage illustrates Sembène's mission, to present an account of what he witnesses and understands to be the realities of African people. By situating himself in a clear historical framework, Sembène seeks to link his own Marxist ideals to a long tradition of African storytelling. He is, in essence, attempting to create a "new griotism" for modern Africa, one that is particularly colored by his own political views. Whereas the griot of the past was an empty vessel into which historical information was poured in order to be accessed by those in power, Sembène calls for a greater sense of "griotic agency" . His work exemplifies the ways in which a griot could use his information for the benefit of not only himself, but the proletariat as well. Whereas the griot of the past was only concerned with his own wellbeing, Sembène's ideal griot uses his information and relates stories for the benefit of the people.

In his seminal work on the portrayal of the griot in contemporary African film, Mbye Cham asserts that Sembène views himself as "the mouth and ears of his people". Moreoever, "prefers to amalgamate, adapt, develop, and enhance certain features of the géwel (griot) and the lekbat (storyteller)." (4). Sembène's amalgamation of griotic traits and functions echoes how he views his mission as a contemporary African artist. By re-interpreting the past role of the griot in his work, he attempts to redefine an idealized role of the modern griot.

Sembène's first film, "Borom Sarret," blatantly critiques the moral corruption of the griot's character. The film's protagonist, a slight, poorly clad cart driver encounters a plump, well-dressed, gold-toothed griot who turns tradition into a tool of exploitation. In order to strip him of his morning's earnings, the griot fabricates a tale about the cart driver's past nobility. The griot's falsified story about the cart driver, which would have been considered authoritative according to Senegalese oral tradition, is presented in stark contrast to the reality of the cart driver's actual social oppression. By placing the griot in his old narrative, Sembène is able to critique the past corruption of this figure in Senegalese society. By criticizing the corrupt modus operandi of the griot of the past, Sembène articulates the characteristics of his vision of West Africa's modern griot: one who values truth, justice, and the good of the people over power and monetary gain.

The figure of the beggar who takes on griotic functions in the film and the novel, "Xala," more accurately describes how Sembène views his role in contemporary society. Though this figure appears in only three scenes, he is an integral part of the narrative. "Xala" is a commentary on a West African nation emerging from it's colonial past, in the process of developing a distorted value system based on money and power. The narrative follows El Hadji, a corrupt member of the African elite, who is stricken with xala, or the curse of impotence. This curse is not only embarrassing for El Hadji, but detrimental to his social standing, as it compromises his role as a powerful member of the emerging nation. The literary narrative is punctuated with scenes in which a street beggar makes his presence known. Though he is never a direct participant in the literary or filmic dialogue, the reader senses his presence throughout the narrative. The following quote sets the tone for how this omnipresent character is represented in both the Xala filmic and literary narratives.

At the corner of the same crowded, busy street, on the right-hand side, the beggar sat cross-legged on his worn-out sheep skin, chanting. Now and again his piercing voice dominated the other noises. Beside him lay a heap of nickel and bronze coins, the gifts of passers-by. (Sembène, trans. Wake 27)

This description of the beggar's "piercing" voice could be taken as a metaphor for the striking messages that habitually stand out in Sembène's work. Though his work is complex and layered, his opinions regarding certain aspects of Senegalese society are clear. During self-reflective moments for El Hadji, especially those regarding the xala in relation to his social standing, the beggar's chant appears, seemingly out of nowhere. An example of this is found in the following quote:

El Hadji: 'I'll be Frank, I can't even manage an erection with the girl. Yet when I left the shower I was stiff. Then when I got to her, nothing. Nothing at all.' The President sat with his mouth open, unable to utter a sound. The beggar's chant, almost as if it were inside the room, rose an octave. (29)

After postulating that the xala was caused by his second wife, El Hadji realizes that is was in fact the beggar who put the curse on him. In a moralistic speech regarding land, clan rights, and corruption of the nation's new power, the beggar informs El Hadji that he cursed him because El Hadji had stolen land that was rightfully his. After acting as quiet observer for years, the beggar finally takes a stance against the distorted value system of the nouvelle-bourgeoisie and proclaims the truth regarding what he has witnessed. His speech is, in essence, a request of his fellow downtrodden members of society to take action against the corruption perpetuated by those in power. The novel ends with a grotesque scene in which the beggar and his indigent companions take turns spitting on the naked torso of El Hadji. Perhaps needless to say, this biting social commentary provoked a fair share of negative response from the Senegalese bourgeoisie at the time of the film's first screening.

The aforementioned characteristics of the beggar mirror Sembène's own griot technique. Like the beggar, Sembène observes the truth about Senegalese society and conveys those aspects, through various media, to a wider audience. In the case of Sembène, he calls for solidarity among artists, intellectuals, and the general population in order to effect change in his adolescent nation. The extreme action taken by the destitute members of society at the end of "Xala" speaks to the potent and controversial messages presented by Sembène regarding the intricacies of the formation of nationhood in Senegal. By exposing the truth regarding the monetary and moral corruption of the nouvelle-bourgeoisie, Sembène lessens their power within the societal framework, thus imposing a xala of sorts on the ruling class.

Another important aspect of the role of the traditional griot is the celebratory function. The griot is present at all major events to observe and preserve the history of the moment, while performing traditional songs and stories about those involved in the ceremony. At the wedding of El Hadji and N'Gone, his third wife, N'Gone's Badyen takes on the role of the griot. The Badyen, a Wolof term meaning maternal aunt, is traditionally in charge of planning the wedding and taking care of the entertainment. The term badyena also takes on a broader meaning of female solidarity and inclusion within the

Senegalese cultural context. The celebratory griotic function appears in the following quote: "The Badyen's joy knew no bounds. She intoned the praises of the family lineage, backed by the female griots, who took up the chorus" (11). In the same way, Sembène praises certain aspects of Senegalese culture in his work, a specific example being the celebration of strong women within Senegalese society takes place in the film "Faat Kiné."

"Faat Kiné" is the story of a single mother, raising two children from different fathers. Through a series of flashbacks and vignettes, Sembène portrays the hardship that the protagonist, Faat Kiné, has faced – from the conception of her first child before she passed her baccalauréat exam to the graduation party of her two children eighteen years later. The revealing conversations between Faat Kiné and her two best friends are not only entertaining, they also expose the concerns, fears and desires of this group of middle-aged Senegalese women. Through their discussions and actions, Sembène celebrates the joie de vivre and strength of the protagonist and her two female companions.

One cannot discuss the role of the griot without examining the tools used to tell the story. We use the term "tools" to refer to both the media Sembène uses to express his ideas about Senegalese society and the language used in his work. As previously mentioned, as a modern griot, Sembène is primarily concerned with truth and realism in his work. Concerning his choice of media, both the written word and film lend themselves to particular types of realism. Issues surrounding this notion arise in the adaptation of the novel Xala into a film. In the novel, there are numerous explicit scenes that refer to El Hadji's flaccid member and his various attempts at having intercourse with his wives. However, the film only hints at such problems. In the film, instead of seeing the flaccid penis, the audience observes El Hadji looking into his pants and looking up with a horrified expression on his face. Whereas the written word has the potential to be more verbally explicit (and therefore realistic), film has the potential to present visual images that can make a significant visual impact on the viewer. A specific example is the scene between El Hadji and the beggar at the end of Xala. In the book, the ending scene reads as follows:

Methodically, El Hadji unbuttoned his pyjama jacket. The first spittle struck him in the face. 'You must not wipe it off.' Adja Awa Astou lowered her eyes. She was crying. A female cripple pushed her and said coarsely: 'Spit if you want him to stuff you again.'... El Hadji's face was running with spittle. He had taken off his pyjama trousers. They were passed around from hand to hand like a trophy. The man who had taken the wedding crown placed it on El Hadji's head. The tumult grew louder... (103)

The scene is certainly disturbing to read, but not half as disturbing as seeing it played out in the film: The beggars are filthy, with missing teeth and gnarled bodies. When they slap Adja and Rama, the sound is so loud and painful that it makes the audience cringe and flinch. The level of shame and disgust associated with the spitting is elevated by the somber, almost contemplative expression on El Hadji's face. The visual transformation of this character, from a powerful businessman to a victim of xala and social oppression, is striking. At the end of the scene, as the "tumult" grows louder, the camera begins to circle the room, disorienting the viewer and putting him or her in the place of El Hadji. At one point, the camera is actually in the middle of the room where El Hadji would be standing, and the beggars are spitting into the camera lens.

When reading this scene, one does not feel this same juxtaposition with El Hadji. The graphic nature of the spittle is especially nauseating. Each yellow mass of coagulated saliva hits the torso of El Hadji with a slap and slides down to his waist. The film ends on a frozen frame, with El Hadji standing in the middle of the room and spittle flying through the air.

An important issue regarding Sembène's choice of media is syndication and distribution. Sembène, along with various other postcolonial writers, including Camara Laye, mentioned earlier in this study, were encouraged by certain French publishing houses to create work exemplifying a typified "Africa". Not wanting to fall into the old role of the griot, by using his body of information to create work for the benefit of another more "powerful" than he, Sembène chose to use this opportunity as a chance to convey his own ideas about Africa to a wider European audience. Ironically, similar to the old griot, Sembène had to create his original work in a media that would be lucrative enough to allow him to continue creating work. As a result, by writing in French for a Western audience, Sembène was excluding a large portion of the proletariat about and for whom he was writing. If Sembène wanted his work to be recognized by his own people, he had to create it in an appropriate media. Which brings us to the question of language.

In the case of Sembène's socio-political context, the question of language is of great significance. All of his novels are written in French, with the exception of certain phrases or terms left in Wolof. However, his films are created in both French and Wolof. Obviously, if his first books were being published in France, they had to be written in French. However, what can one make of his subsequent use of both French and Wolof in his film work? Is this a political move, or purely pragmatic? In a 2002 interview with Nicole Aas-Rouxparis, Sembène addresses this point:

Q: Parlons de la langue. Quel est aujourd'hui votre rapport à la langue française? Je pense par exemple aux échanges entre Rama et son père dans Xala au sujet de wolof et du français.

Q: Let's talk about languages. Today, what is your relationship to the French language? I am thinking, for example, about the exchanges between Rama and her father in Xala regarding the use of Wolof vs. French.

R: L'Europe est en retard sur l'évolution de l'Afrique à ce sujet. La langue est un produit de politique. Ce sont les hommes au gouvernement qui décident de cette politique. A mon avis, toutes les langues recèlent de la richesse. Cela depend de qui les emploie et comment on les emploie. Dans nos écoles, au Sénégal, nous enseignons toutes les langues européenes. Nous écrivons aussi dans les langues africaines, et nous avons même traduit la Bible et le Coran. Personellement, je ne veux pas qu'on nous enferme dans la francophonie.

A: Europe is behind on the evolution of Africa regarding this subject. Language is a product of politics. The government officials are the ones who decide this. In my opinion, all languages are full of richness. It depends on who uses them and how they use them. In our schools, in Senegal, we teach all of the European languages. We also write in African languages, and we have even translated the Bible and the Koran. Personally, I don't think that we should enclose ourselves in a strictly French speaking environment/limit ourselves to the French language. (Aas-Rouxparis 577) (Author's translation)

The scene in "Xala," to which Aas-Rouxparis refers, is particularly revelatory regarding Sembène's own linguistic views. Rama, the eldest daughter of El Hadji, joins a political group at the university, and insists on only speaking Wolof with her family and her fiancé. Her polemical views do not match those of El Hadji, and he ends up beating her and prohibits the use of Wolof in the home. This scene is Sembène's commentary on the nouvelle bourgeoisie's obvious disdain for and rejection of the mother tongue in favor of the colonizer's father tongue. From a pragmatic point of view, Sembène also recognizes that one cannot completely abandon French, as it is the language of politics and business. He explains his point of view in the following quote from the Rouxparis interview:

83

Q. Mais, vous, vous avez écrit vos romans en français, vous avez fait vos films en français ou en langues nationales avec les sous-titres. Vous avez fait un choix pour communiquer avec votre publique.

Q: But you wrote your novels in French, you directed your films in French or in the national language with subtitles. You made a choice in order to communicate with your public.

R: Je n'ai pas fait de choix! J'ai un outil et je l'utilise. Les langues sont un moyen qui nous permet de communiquer, c'est tout. Savez-vous qu'à l'heure actuelle il y a beaucoup plus de professeurs qui parlent français et anglais sans compter leur langue africaine- aux Etats-Unis qu'en Europe?

A: I didn't make a choice! I have a tool and I use it. Languages are a means of communication, that's all. Did you know that at this very moment there are many more professors who speak French and English, not counting their African language, in the United States than in Europe? (Aas-Rouzparis, 577) (Author's translation)

While his first statement was more ideological, this quote reflects Sembène's pragmatism concerning the use of language in his work. He recognizes the political structure for what it is, and works within the system to make his message heard. His films, namely "Xala," and "Faat Kiné," were created using both French and Wolof. "Faat Kiné" is a particularly interesting study on his systematic use of both languages, and a realistic representation of speech patterns that would actually occur in Senegalese society. In this case Sembène uses both languages in order to fulfill his griotic mission of realistic representation.

In the opening scene, Faat Kiné, a member of the nouvelle bourgeoisie, speaks French with the clients in her gas station. She receives a phone call later on in the day from her daughter, explaining that her daughter passed her baccalauréat exam. Again, Kiné speaks French on the phone. French dominates the first thirty minutes of the film until Kiné's daughter returns from school and interacts with her grandmother and the domestique. Here, they all speak Wolof together. When Kiné returns, she speaks Wolof with the grandmother and French with her two children.

This is perhaps the most linguistically revelatory scene in the film. Kiné speaks Wolof to her mother out of respect for tradition, and the fact that her mother most likely prefers speaking in Wolof to speaking in French. The viewer learns early in the film that Faat Kiné is a strong, skilled woman who is dedicated to the advancement of her children. She speaks French to them to encourage their academic and professional development. A pragmatist to the end, Kiné knows that the educational system and the business world both operate in French. If her children are to succeed, they must be comfortable with this language.

It is fascinating to observe how Kiné's demeanor changes as she switches between the two languages. French is her language of business. When she is speaking French, even to her children, her posture is very straight and her chin is tilted up. When she is speaking Wolof with her mother, she is often lounging on the sofa, lighting up a cigarette, or in one scene, even removing her uncomfortable undergarments. Likewise, she speaks Wolof with her two friends as they slouch in their seats, sip drinks and speak freely about personal subjects such as relationships, sex, AIDS, and children.

In following with Sembène's penchant for realism, it is clear that the film "Ceddo" is entirely in Wolof. "Ceddo" is a political commentary on the expansion of Islam throughout Senegal. The film is set in rural Senegal in the 19th century. Considering the film's setting, it is logical why Sembène would choose to set this film in Wolof. During the 19th century, French was primarily spoken in the larger colonial cities, such as St. Louis or Dakar, and not in smaller settlements or rural communities. Sembène's choice to use Wolof in "Ceddo" further reinforces his role as a "realist" griot. As Balufu Bakupa-Kanyinda states in his article on African cinema, entitled "Challenging Stereotypes":

To produce a film in Africa is an act of resistance. It is about looking at the world's stories and giving one's opinion about them, capturing and inquiring about collective memory, attracting, entertaining, and informing. It is also about making Africans realize that cinema is a powerful tool for development. (1)

This quote succinctly articulates what Sembène attempts to accomplish in his work as a modern day griot. His work reflects what he understands to be the reality of his country and inspires his compatriots to change and improve the nation's sociopolitical climate. The films "Borom Sarret," "Xala," and "Faat Kiné" provide a clear framework in which to examine the ways, both blatant and subtle, in which Sembène redefines the role of the griot in contemporary society. In addition, the content and narrative techniques used by Sembène fulfill his Marxist vision of what the modern griot should strive to accomplish in his work, a realistic portrayal of the various experiences of Senegalese men and women. Sembène's use of language mimics this self-consciously constructed artistic and political position. As we have seen, he uses Wolof in his films and novels to preserve the "realistic" qualities of his narratives. However, his use of French is a clear choice to inscribe himself within the larger community of la francophonie, comprising not only fellow African authors, but also myriad postcolonial voices around the globe.

Chapter 5

Oral Multidimensional Collage in Recent Fiction

O. Okuyade

> The past remains locked away unless it can be re-
> visualized, taken up at another level, rehearsed
> profoundly at another level to release new
> implications, a new kind of thrust. (Wilson Harris:
> "Literacy and the imagination.")

Constructing Alter-Cultures:

THE African novel remains undoubtedly a
foundational site where African writers continue to
interrogate the conflictual relationship between mankind
and the cosmos. Universally, man continues to grapple
with his existence as a stranger in a world characterized
by metaphysical problems and the spiritual aridity of
man's inability to explain the interface between the
terrestrial and celestial worlds. Man's continuous search
for the meaning of life remains inconclusive, and as such
writers have continued to experiment with their art in
order to resolve mankind's most elusive question: why

are we here? The three texts chosen for analysis in this essay: Chin Ce's The Visitor, Phaswane Mpe's Welcome To Our Hillbrow, and Biyi Bandele-Thomas' The man who came in from the back of Beyond are vibrant contributions to the ongoing dialogue – why are we here? Ce's other oeuvres like Bandele-Thomas' have attracted robust attention. However, their novels mentioned above continue to suffer inexplicable neglect. This may be attributed to the form and structure of the novels. The few commentaries on these three novels locate them within postmodern and postcolonial traditions. Reading these texts from this bifocal dimension is understandable, especially because of their thematic kinship. The writers seem to structure their plots around postmodern tenets and have drawn from the consistent repertoire of common post colonial themes: Africa's permanent burdens, the ubiquity of corruption and violence in postcolonial Africa, the debility of the voiceless masses, the irrelevance of government, and the continuous search for an alternative for the failed systems. The texts equally explore the on-going cultural confrontation between foreign and indigenous traditions in post colonial Africa. The post colonial issues highlighted above are not nascent in African literature but they are of monumental importance and as such they remain issues African writers have repeatedly and continuously explored. Invariably, it is rather difficult to argue that these novels inaugurate new themes for African literature. However, if one turns away from issues bordering on thematic context and content, thereby turning the search light on issues of technicalities and form, one can arguably contend that these texts depart from the ordinary, predictable and routine. Each of these narratives demonstrates a remarkable sense of formal experimentation and they have tactically extended, progressively, the writers creative exploration of multiple literary styles, genres, traditions and the multidimensionality of perspectives. These writers in revisiting popular postcolonial themes have created cultural alternatives thereby finding extraordinary new modes in expressing familiar and familial issues, given them greater insight, imagination and complexity.

By reflecting on new openings and ongoing developments in African literature, literary theory and culture we seem to point beyond post modernism and raise a fundamental question whether what appears as newness is not rather a return to traditional concepts, theoretical premises and authorial practices. These writers, Ce in particular, weave incredibly together science fiction and mysticism, history and myth, truth and fiction, philosophy and literature. Our concern here is, therefore, to examine the complexities and significance of the interweaving of these discourses in the novels. As stated earlier, these texts are usually read as postcolonial and postmodern but this is a transpolar reading. Though the novels are postcolonial and postmodern, the narratological devices employed in the texts cast them within the mould of the modern. Jean-Francois Lyotard in The Postmodern Condition: A Report on Knowledge defines modern as a term:

To designate any science that legitimates itself with reference to metadisocurse (....) making an explicit appeal to some grand narrative, such as the dialectics of spirit, the hermeneutics of meaning, the emancipation of the rational or working subject, or the creating of wealth. (xiii)

The postulation above makes bare the authorizing essence for the legitimacy of knowledge which finds its base in the metaphysical tradition and its notion of truth as it relates to concepts of totality and the certitude of an absolute subject.

It may seem a little incredible to attempt a harmonization of these texts under a singular theoretical channel and pursue a reading methodology that will tie the texts in a similar conceptual frame. The most fascinating similarity in these novels is the demise of the protagonists in the first couple of pages of the novels. Invariably, if a protagonist dies in the first chapter of a narrative how can the plot be propagated without a central character whose life the entire narrative is woven around? The novels equally strike a similarity in the recurrence of certain motifs. They include: revenge, journey, smoking and drugging and suicide, and the story telling motif. The books are equally woven around the theme of self-actualization which is only realizable if the individual looks inward, that is, the possibility of finding the divine within oneself rather than communicated through intermediaries such as priests, saints or the church. These writers have constructed a space for the negotiation of identity which has been imagined in a number of ways, through a number of metaphors, deployment of symbols, especially sex symbols. Two of the texts, The Visitor and The man who came in from the back of Beyond, have employed the metaphors of science fiction and the doctrine and concept of New Ageism. One other fascinating feature of these texts is role changing. The protagonists are sometimes active subjects and, eventually, they end up as passive witnesses. These therefore form some of the theoretical issues examined in this essay.

In order to avoid any form of prolixity, we must not attempt an intertextual reading of these texts to articulate how these writers exploit oral resources in their works but choose to achieve our purpose through narratology. This methodological channel will equally indicate the significance of narrative theory and method in the study of the modern African novel.

Given our African literary aesthetic, cultural and social history, realist fiction hardly fascinates some of us who obtain immense pleasure from reading transformative novels that employ spiritual realism. Ce's The Visitor is an eloquent example. These three texts challenge the reader's preconceptions of narrative form and content. They challenge foundational understandings of memory, society and identity. As already indicated, these writers engage in similar projects which may hardly be discernable from an intertextual and theoretical perspective.

A contrapuntal reading will no doubt enable the location of these projects. John Christie argues that the play of narrative forms, the play between modernist and postmodernist narrative styles, ideally suits and enable these writers to "shock readers into new ways of perceiving the world" (12). However, despite one's fascination with these challenging novels, most students encounter great difficulties in approaching and understanding these non-realist novels. So we often burn so much time interrogating their aesthetics and how they affect their reception of a novel, especially a difficult one. These writers challenge and subvert traditional narrative practices. Nevertheless the forms of the narrative practice the writers adopt render the texts difficult to assimilate. The novels, especially that of Ce and Bandele-Thomas, therefore situate within the tradition of science fiction genre, spirito-mystical realism, and modernism because of the multi-factorial layers of setting and multidimensionality of perspectives and characterization. Our task is to examine the ways in which these writers' application of the conventions of spirito-mystical realism, modernism and science fiction enable their social and cultural commentaries.

The written mode of literature continues to be privileged above the oral when issues bordering on the interconnection between both are discussed. Although, Ian Watt in The Rise of the Novel, has contended that the cardinal distinguishing feature of the novel is its "formal realism" through which the novel presents a full and authentic report of human experience converged "through a more largely referential use of language" (32), African writers have continued to stretch the limits of the concept of realism. Reality in the context of the African novel is hazy and ontologically nebulous and because of this indefiniteness, African writers explore the concept by questioning the interaction between the fantastic and the mundane. This argument is not a rebuttal of Watt, but suggests that the concept is relative. Wole Soyinka suggests that the African ritual archetype is one born through the archetype's withdrawal "into an inner world

93

from which he returns communicating a new strength for action" (33). Thus realism for the African writer, as in Ce's and Bandele-Thomas' deployment of dreams, is an extension of the material and the transcendental.

Re-membering the Spiritual Order: Chin Ce: The Visitor

The Visitor begins with a prologue which aptly captures the politics of crime and enrichment and the profits of violence. Violence and crimes in Africa are not an indication of instability or a breakdown of constitutional order but these phenomena have become tools for constituted authority to sustain their positions and hold the voiceless masses around the marginal space of passivity and silence, because the major strategy for their continuous stay in power is the brutal efficiency with which they consolidate power. Thus violence is a formidable instrument for the rulers to consolidate themselves in government, thereby compromising their commitment to the ruled whom they use as object for the orchestration of violence and crimes, especially as a chaotic ambience will not make room for any form of development. Crime and violence are gradually becoming formidable tools for bureaucratic power. As Patrick Chabel and Jean-Pascal Daloz argue:

There is undeniably in Africa today a high level of violence- not just in situations where law and order have broken down entirely but also where conditions are deemed to be relatively stable. Indeed, there are now very few countries on the continent where brutality does not

94

encroach directly on the daily lives of ordinary Africans as they go about their business. Or rather, the business of living and working, especially in cities (and Africa continues to urbanize at a frightening pace), is increasingly fraught with the danger of suffering violence and crime. (77)

The above argument reveals the burden of existence and anxiety in living in Aja -a society that is run from a monolithic dimension, both economically and socio-politically. The Ironi cult power rests on the laps of members of this criminally minded organization that produces the leadership of the society. The cult possesses infinite powers to alter any situation to its favour. Though, Mensa, the protagonist is a member of this powerful cult, he seems to negotiate his life around the margins; he is just an ordinary help hand. A university drop out whose only means of survival is to function as an instrument for the orchestration of crimes and violence. His membership is only utilitarian and it functions to solidify and consolidate the place of the leaders of the cult like Chief Jaguda and facilitate their social ascendancy or advancement in the socio-political ladder of an ailing society. Mensa muses on his plight as they await goods from one of their piratic escapades.

This was the dirty part of the job which no public official of this land would dare, thought Mensa wryly. Yet its execution was responsible for the millions that exchanged hands and made millionaires of influential politicians and their allies. (8)

Immediately after this incidence we are introduced to another character Erie, who seems to be lost, to the extent of lacking knowledge of his identity. He knows nothing about himself and the world around him. Invariably, this character is in search of a selfhood larger than mere knowledge of self. Considering Mensa's confession in the prologue prior to the piratical escapade, it becomes clear that Mensa is dead. In Erin land, he is undergoing a process of (re)memory. What could have been responsible for his present form and existence remains a monumental question in the mind of the reader. The confession ends with ellipsis which becomes an artistic scheme Ce uses to demonstrate that the narrative is strictly about remembrance of a punctuated existence. However, this function is not permanent, but a process towards finding the self, a kind of "arrested political maturity, unfulfilled potential and premature failure" (Wright 15). Every other incidence in the novel is recounted through memory. Erie as noted earlier is in a quest to unravel the mystery behind his new state/form -- a search that is likely to lead to spiritual self-actualization which may be occasioned by an awakening. These shifting perspectives may get a reader confused, however, the three major characters: Mensa, Erie and Deego, are one. Amanda Grants insists that since the narrative centres on the politics of recovery "it would be therefore correct to state that the story teller is here concerned with the individuals quest for wholeness (the search for purpose) signified in Erie's lost memory" (25). Before his demise, Mensa is an active subject as protagonist, but in Erin land he becomes a mere observer, because here, his life in Aja begins to unfold before his very eyes so that he may be able to reconcile his past and the present in order to envision the future. To know himself beyond his mortal limitations, the inhabitants of this ancestral spiritual world are to assist him with recollection which can only be realized if Erie looks inward.

Ce's engagements with the ancestral all knowing world is breathtakingly amazing. His exploration of the rhetoric and dialectics of (re)memory and the struggle for self-cum-spiritual actualization are characterized by superfluous descriptions which are almost marred by countless humdrum occurrences. These aspects of the narrative are, arguably, the very point of departure from existing forms and the locus of a redefined aesthetic. This is what Kamon Saldivar describes as "almost total rejection of traditional narrative procedure" (176). Characters like Granddad, Zeta, Uzi and Adaku become the channel through which Erie is to pursue the process of meeting himself while Uzi's house of memory becomes a memorial warehousing where the drama of memory unfolds. Before this process of meeting the self begins one notice Erie observing the unknown:

It plagued him daily to walk about the walls of the city like some disembodied entity, a ghost whose only memory of his identity comes in flashes and hunches. "You are at home among your spirits Zita's granddad told him. 'But you will not understand, and it were better you did not ask too much questions. Take those day dreams, visions and nightmares as natural as the colour of your tan, things which will continue to hold little value to you until you come to face your past in order to know the moment. (22)

Erie is totally alienated. He is present, yet absent. This sense of present absence and alienation are solidly rooted in modernism, issuing from what Douglas Mecabe describes as "a commitment to the life-goods of self fulfillment and the search for authenticity that peculiarly and centrally characterize the modern identity" (9). In order to come to terms with his lost identity, even before his demise -because Mensa's life before the coincidence of the death of his friends, Omo and Sena is characterized by aridity-- this foregrounds an identity in dire need of spiritual rearmament. This emptiness stems from the greedy and gluttonous activities of people like Chief Jaguda and the discourteousness and the restlessness that characterize life in Aja. Mensa's death is not important to the narrative, however it becomes the conduit through which he can actualize himself from the isolationisms life and death have constructed for him.

Death automatically becomes a metaphor for a journey. Mensa-Erie embarks on a long metaphysical journey through time, in order to show him knowledge of man's ability to survive and most importantly a self actualization that human beings are gods hidden from themselves. Erie's experiences in the ancestral plain reveal that individuals are not only capable of progressing, they can equally develop the essential capacities of a universal unit -mankind's explosive enemies can be converted into purposive force. As Jose Vasconcelos opines, over time differences will disappear and a "fifth universal race will change" (9). This new "synthetic race that shall gather all the treasures of history in order to give expression to universal desire shall be created" (18). Vasconcelos argues further that we shall transform ourselves, and leave behind a material or warlike and "intellectual or political" past and move toward a spiritual or aesthetic future.

In symbolic ways Erin land bears significant resemblance to Vasconcels' borderless system or universalpolis. While his argumentation is premised on the "facts of history and science" (8) in rejection of the fantasy of the novelist, Ce adopts the fictional form grounded in folk culture. The argument of Ce's thematic groundings shall be pursued subsequently. The Visitor becomes an eloquent dramatization of transformational synergy, the synthesis of polar plains, mortal-spiritual, to attain a universal unit and the newly emerging synthetic humans, represent triumph. And this triumph is reflected in the narrative as Erie after the realization of selfhood and the preparatory re-journey out of indefinite time to concrete time.

The shifting perspectives, the triad dimensionality of characterization and the description of Erin land and its wholeness, a system that is a unit, a world that hides nor shelters nothing, signposts the narrative around the high-tech versions of mainstream representations of science fiction as Matrix, Star Trek, Star Wars, The Terminator, Babylon 5, Armageddon. Without any anticipatory doubt though, Ce may have adopted generic tropes of science fiction novel in order to illuminate and speculate the possibilities of a different epistemological and ontological space. Perhaps living in Nigeria, Ce must have experienced many horrible circumstances: the crave for material acquisitions to the exclusion of spiritual development. Erin land affords Ce the opportunity to speculate about social structure, other epistemologies, and other sciences which are not western. Through Erie's metaphorical journey is Erin land, Ce allows us to question our interactions with and acceptances of difference, this is not to insist that this is the dominant element in the novel. Ce as a writer always fantasizes on "what an ideal society should look like" (Okuyade 173), just as he does with his concise exploration of the ant community in Children of Koloko. While Erin – the alternative model of existence – allows us to question our models and metaphors for understanding the world around us, this is not the dominant either. The exposition of Erin land as another socio-spiritual other or model is arguably, the most significant feature of the narrative – what we do in life echoes in eternity and most importantly, no matter the blemishes of the past and the present, the future remains untainted without any blemish.

It is quite interesting that Ce in attempting to envision and articulate alternatively social cum spiritual structures turns to an indigenous past located in the oral mode, where tales are replete with the beauty of the after life. Ce draws from popular oral motif. The title of the novel is a signification of this motif; the temporality of mortal existence. In fact the entire narrative is woven around a philosophical Igbo traditional folk song which appears before the story:

We are visitors upon the earth
This world is not our own

We have come but to a market place
Only to purchase and go home. (5)

This is indeed what gives the narrative its oral temper. Moreover, if a critic or an artist is attempting to imagine an alternative to Africa's current socio-political failures, they should look ahead into the future like Ce advocates - a synthesis of the folk tradition and sets of metaphors located within the locality of the concept of New Ageism and science fiction. In this sense, it could be argued that Ce foreshadows Donna Haraway's cyborg consciousness: "I'd rather be a cyborg than a goddess" (106). The Visitor becomes Ce's fictional attempt to make mankind see beyond his limited physical self, a kind of transcendence of consciousness. The text is meant to help people actualize their inner selves and thereby bring about a perfect co-existence, not only the inhabitants of the world, but between the individual and his/her yearning for transcendental experience. Ce has artistically advocated the need for man to develop the inner depths, the middle dimension of the human spirit. This is what Maccabe describes as "the semi-divine sides of our nature that we need to actualize and express and reconnect with in other to be truly free" (11). The true path of social harmony and justice, socio-economic anticipation and inner peace is neither in capitalism espoused by Chief Jaguda, the strong man of Ironi, nor in social rebellion embarked upon by Mensa, Omo and Sena, but rather in spiritual path of quietude, introspection, magical perception, and the journey of self actualization undertaken by Erie.

Mensa, Erie and Deego are paradigmatic of mankind's experience as an incarnate spirit progressing, many reincarnations, towards attaining spiritual perfection. The relationship between these characters aptly demonstrates that self realization is not a fixed destination but a process without closure. The Visitor is a philosophical treatise with multiple perspectives and characterization; it appears the book celebrates the concept of New Ageism, especially as Erie begins his spiritual life and ends his mortal existence through a rupture of his identity and his past. All he remembers is the bang which transits and translates him into a new form of existence. This rupture doubles the genealogical break suffered in his previous life. He remembers nothing and can tell nothing of himself and origins. The reader meets him in search of buried vestiges of a lost consciousness that can only be retrieved by looking inward in order to reconcile the past with the present. Nasrin Qader makes glaring the relational opposition of present-past and past-present when he remarks that:

This is not a past that was at one point a present; it is not a historical past, but rather a pastness per se, the erasure of presence. It is what separates presence from itself, a kind of spacing without memory. What makes memory possible is an essential disjointedness in time (13).

The fragmentation of the narratology and the achronological arrangement of plot make the text a difficult read. However, Deego's perspective, which resides in the space of contamination between dream and reality, sleep and wakefulness, redeems the book from mere fantasy. After all, the entire narrative is indeed a dream: Deego dozes off in the middle of a midnight movie which runs into his psychic networking and launches a dream in his subconscious. As long as it is a dream, the text becomes realistic, because the world of dream has no borders or limitations. However the most fascinating feature of the novel is that "Ce explores the other world" (Okuyade "Locating" 155), which only exists in the imagination. But most importantly The Visitor reasserts the popular epistemological belief that death is not an end, it is a process for the furtherance of the self beyond the imagined and predictable. The text inscribes death, according to Qader,

within a dialogical logic where it becomes identified as a moment of negativity within the system, as an intermediary stage towards the subject's self fulfillment. The overcoming of death is a requirement for the dialectical process to function, allowing meaning to appropriate non-meaning, memory to ensure the fulfillment of signification, and life to assert its supremacy with the mastery of the "I". Literature then becomes the scene of this completion. (19)

The Visitor is characterized throughout by an adoption and a translation, as flamboyant as it is skilful, of themes, topoi, events, characters, images and above all rhetorical and metaphorical strategies from both the written mode and the folk tradition. The Visitor becomes a paradigm of an African text which espouses the concept of spirito-mystical realism. This is discernable from its multiple fantasies, its navigation of polar worlds and its introduction of the supernatural into the everyday or mundane. Like the other two novels, we are exposed to characters that are fatally crushed by their obsessions, and above all in the apocalyptic vision of the diminution of the youth population. Ce's biggest asset lies in his ability to construct tales of enduring meanings from apparently mundane situations. His narrative may generate confusion, especially because of the shifting perspectives and the rhetorical strategies he adopts but The Visitor is certainly distinct, profound and innovative. The narrative suggests layers of inexplicable emotion which signposts the place of memory in the eternal search for the self. Invariably, through the power of memory, Ce peripherises the past, making the future hegemonic, because no matter how vibrant the past is, the future remains ultimately important especially as it gives meaning to it --without a future the past is inconsequential. Thus, Ce makes the future memorably bold even before it is experienced and ensures the relevance of the past is not compromised. He realizes this through the rhetoric of (re)memory and the ontological grounding of folk tradition.

The Infinite-Omniscient Self-review: Phaswane Mpe: Welcome to our Hillbrow

Like Ce's The Visitor, Welcome to Our Hillbrow prioritizes heavily on memory in order to interrogate the past and present to enable a negotiable future. The novel is a vibrant expression of the virility and innovativeness of South African literature, especially as some critics doubt if anything vibrant can emerge form the post-apartheid context. The novel is a multi-layered dystopian narrative which captures the anxiety of a post-apartheid society. The text engages issues that characterize a society emerging from the threshold of racial tensions. The dominant moods of such societies are suspicion and fear.

The narrative x-rays problems of HIV-AIDS and xenophobia and the plight of Makwerekwere (migrants). The issues Mpe engages within the novel remain very current but we must move beyond thematic engagements and content to the cardinal concern with stories and how they are told. This will in turn help in locating the story-telling devices employed in the novel within the oral tradition. The novel creates an ambience where one assesses individual lives as an unfolding story configured through a linear temporal sequence. The novel appears to be rebutting the popular notion that art imitates or represents life; the way characters are portrayed seems to reflect the other way round. Richard Kearney's discussion of the suppleness of narrative is particularly of immense importance when considering Mpe's novel. Kearney argues that, "every human existence is a life in search of a narrative" and "narrativity is what marks, organizes and clarifies temporal experience" (129). This remark is very important to the text, especially as the protagonist's life flashes before his very eyes though in an immortal position. There are two interrelated tropes which strike unique kinship with Ce's and Bandele-Thomas' novels, and which Mpe explores explicitly. These tropes rather help man to define his position in life as a soul in search of something he hardly knows, and this search is what sustains him in his most depressing moments – life as a story, and life as a journey. Our lives can be appraised as "part of an unfolding life story" and each life story cries out to be imitated, that is transformed into the story of a life" (Kearney 131). Through these tropes one can better appreciate the narratological devices Mpe employs to render the story of fear, anxiety and suspicion.

The novel employs very formidable oral devices which are not very popular among African writers. Besides drawing from Africa's folkloric pool – the story telling tradition, Mpe reflects the role that story-telling continues to play in contemporary South Africa and Africa at large – how stories are distorted, adjusted and readjusted. This aspect of the novel is a signpost of the importance of one of the unique features of oral literature, which is performance. The others are: the audience which is an essential factor in the realization of an oral product, and occasion. Performance and the audience are of immense importance to this discourse and shall be examined for their relevance to the text.

The novel begins with a stunning and direct address, however the addressee/protagonist is already dead: "If you were still alive, Refentse, child of Tragolong, you would be glad that Bafana Bafana lost to France in the 1998 soccer World Cup fiasco" (1). This is the most striking feature of orality in this text; an anonymous narrator explicitly addresses Refentse through the mode of direct address, to an already dead protagonist. Mpe's style is characterized by a most unusual literary device, especially within the context of African literature. This is no doubt the most fascinating aspect of the text; it actually takes the form of a prosopopoeia, a direct address to the dead. The addressee is infinitely absent yet he has another opportunity to explore and appraise life from this infinite vantage position. The novel is thus narrated from the second person, rather than in the usual and familiar first or third person. This device creates a space for the reader who is not just an audience but automatically becomes the addresser. This has the uncanny effect of evoking while at the same time confirming the absolute absence of the dead addressee and the distant addresser (the reader) and the immediate addresser – the narrator.

From the narratology, especially the participatory mode which affords the reader a space within the story, one can contend that Mpe, is dually drawing from an oral story-telling tradition, and reflecting the role that story-telling continues to play in contemporary African society. The novel reworks and reconstructs Refentse's life-story, and other life-stories which intersect with his, in particular Refilwe's. Through authorial distancing, the narrator artistically synthesizes desperate events and weaves together the many stories that collectively constitute the novel.

The retrospective mode of the narration gives the novel an elegiac dimension. Like a film, Refentse's life is relayed specifically to re-interrogate his death and other deaths remotely and immediately related to his death. Through this perspective, Refentse is afforded another opportunity to watch the drama of life unfold before his very eyes. However on this occasion, he only observes just like Erie in The Visitor from the vantage position of the all knowing world which is heaven in the case of Refentse, while Erie's is the ancestral world. From this position the protagonist is able to look back on his life while on earth with the benefit of retrospect, omniscience and conscience to understand that his dubious escape from life through suicide is pointless. Through the process of relaying the past, the narrative brings into play two contrasting perspectives – that of addressee-observer from the vantage point of heaven, and that of mere mortals, the audience on earth, who are limited in knowledge of their existence. Invariably, through authorial distancing, the narrator brings to the fore man's limitations and makes very pertinent the infinity of the after-life and the power of omniscience of the ancestral world. With the benefit of retrospection, the narrator makes Refentse acknowledge the fact that he is a killer; he is responsible for the other deaths connected to his. His brief affair with Bohlale and his eventual suicide is responsible for Bohlale's death, Sammy's madness, and for the deaths of his own mother and Lerato's. Although he does not create the chain reactions of all these deaths intentionally, he realizes his culpability in the entire process. The narrator makes this point very glaring with the mode of the direct address:

You have since come to learn the facts, because Heaven affords you the benefit of retrospect and omniscience. Heaven, you now know, is not some far-off place where God sits in judgement, waiting to read out his endless, cruel list of offenders on Earth. This Heaven that is your present abode is a very different thing. It carries within it its own Hell. You understand now that you are, in fact, a killer. You killed yourself. And unintentionally, you have also killed your own mother. (47)

The excerpt above indicates that the narrator's non-judgmental and compassionate attitude coupled with the direct address mode, crumbles the diurnal space between narration and action. It bequeaths the novel with an immediacy of dialogic interaction, which as noted earlier equally incorporates the reader into the story as a participant and audience.

The relevance of this narrative style lies in the fact that it is difficult for one to fully understand the significance of an experience when he or she is in the midst of it. While a gap between experience and narration is desirable because it allows for analysis and, by extension, agency, it also limits the authority of the protagonist because the reader's perception of the subject self is shaped primarily by the narrator's assessment and attitude.

From Refentse's perspective, the novel engages with very serious ethical issues especially that of tolerance. Migrants in Hillbrow are not given opportunity for survival; they are not welcome because Tiragalong and Hillbrowans feel there must be something weird about them as nothing good comes out of any union with them. However, the narrator's non-judgemental and compassionate attitude, with its implicit plea for tolerance, rationality, understanding and forgiveness, contrasts starkly with the views attributed to the residents of Tiragalong or Hillbrow and provides a normative ethical frame for the narrative. This generous and compassionate view of human life is one which Refentse and Refiliwe ultimately come to share. As he observes mortals from Heaven, Refentse wishes that he possessed the power to make Tiragalong adjust their perception of life, especially the fact that "Refilwe was only doing what we all did: searching for meaning and happiness in life" (Mpe: 111). He equally comes to appreciate one fact Refilwe learns only through the process of her journey from home, that every (wo)man is a potential Makwerewere. The plot structure of the novel is designed to tell Refentse's story in such a way that instead of reinforcing prejudice and superstition, it promotes tolerance and understanding.

On the whole, the entire narrative is geared towards adjusting stories told about Refentse especially his mother's gruesome murder by the sympathizers who are of the opinion that she bewitched her child. The novel makes very emphatic that as our lives can be seen as narratives where we are key players, so also our lives could be relived after death in the memories of others through stories they tell of us. This aspect of the novel strikes a similarity with Bandele-Thomas' novel.

Like The Visitor, death is not total annihilation, but an access to Heaven, the world of continuous existence, which Roy Faylard opines is "located in the memory and consciousness of those who live with us and after us" (93). It becomes the memorial bank where people visit and revisit, exhuming and burning, adjusting or refining the lived stories. Invariably they are not totally uncorrupted version of any story, so Trigalong now is going to do same to Refilwe who has helped in adjusting Refentse's own story.

The novel presents the rural shadows in the city as part of the complicated intertwining of meaning and identity in this exciting and dangerous city. In "Our Hillbrow", none of Mpe's characters survive like those of Ce in the first narrative perspective, yet the novel has a kind of elegiac temper which itself is a testament of the city's fascination and presence in the contemporary imaginary. It appears nobody survives this city. The survivor is not human. It is far from the young struggling characters in the narrative. It is a human product, the story and this is what gives these characters their redemption – tales will be woven around their lives. Besides the illustration of the virility of fictional storytelling, the novel suggests that by engaging the art of storytelling, "whether as writer or reader, narrator or auditor" (Gayland: 3), one may be better positioned to contemplate the agonizing complexities of the burden of humanity. As noted earlier the novel demonstrates the importance of one of the issues relating to performance --verbal variability, the other is improvisation, which is not too relevant to this study. By verbal variability, we mean no tale has only a single version. Each oral performer or story teller introduces his own words, phrases, demeanor, and other stylistic devices. No two story tellers can tell the same story using exactly the same words or narrative patterns in the act of rendition. There is no fixity about the use of language in oral tradition. It is in this regard that oral literature differs significantly from other forms of literary art especially the written mode. It is therefore impossible to insist on an authentic version of a tale. This is the most captivating aspect of Mpe's novel; it is like a treatise on the elasticity and variability of oral tales. Like The

Visitor, Welcome to Our Hillbrow is characterized by a triad dimensionality which is "reportorially executed, and the narrative incidents are projected within triad topographical spaces of the city of Johannesburg, the village of Tiragalong, and Oxford" (Ezeliora 113-114). Refentse's story is told from different dimensions, until Refilwe supplies her own version which she insists is the authentic one because it is narrated from the inside about the inside. At death, Refilwe's story will equally be configured; it will provoke numerous versions. Thus, human life remains the most powerful source of tales because it creates opportunity for mankind to continue to audit and edit the self and the society bringing to bear the moralistic and didactic power of stories.

Story-telling and Self-editing: Biyi Bandele-Thomas: The Man who came in from the Back of Beyond

The Man who came in from the Back of Beyond differs from the first two novels already discussed in this essay, although the protagonist re-edits himself, like the protagonist of first two novels, he does not die in order to appreciate life from the all-knowing perspective. However, the unfolding drama of another protagonist, in the third perspective of the narrative affords the young Lakemf the luxury of knowing and realizing himself. This process of self realisation takes the form of an Orphic journey, realized through his literature teacher's uncompleted manuscript and the verbal tales which supplies the missing middle of the narrative. Lakemf visits his literature teacher on a weekend. Rather than allow him sit idly in his room while he busied with his garden, he gives him the uncompleted manuscript of his novel. Reading becomes a trope for socio-cultural searching in the narrative, especially as it creates the space for the transformation of the protagonist. What appears to be the most fascinating feature of this text is the multiplicity of perspectives and the act of story telling. Elsewhere we contended that the "narrative is scattered and fragmented. Bandele-Thomas uses the first person multiple narrative technique. This is highlighted by the presence of the voice of Lakemf, Maude, Yau, Mitchell Socrates and of course that of Bozo Macika in the text" (Modernist 64). The novel like Ce's The Vistor is narrated from three different perspectives, at the first narrative level; the "I-witness" is used by Lakemf to describe his literature teacher Maude:

The very first time I saw him I had the distinct but unfathomable impression that I was starring at a man on his way to the gallows...he taught literature and English in the fifth form but what we really learn from him, although he never knew it, was that if one spent one's days and night writing verses and perusing books and correcting literature essays from illiterate students one was bound like early man to descend into dotage before the age of thirty. (1)

From the excerpt above, the reader sees Maude through Lakemf's eyes. The second narrative perspective the "I as protagonist" is employed by Maude to narrate his fragmented autobiography which he completes orally because some items are missing from the written form he gives to Lakemf, his students to read. Within Maude's story is another protagonist, Bozo Macika who coincidentally is Maude's girl-friend's ex-boyfriend. The third person omniscient point of view is used in narrating Bozo's story which Maude weaves into a novel. The emphasis at this narrative level falls on the Abednego family which is at the brink of excision, because of their short temper, their inability to keep their feelings in check and the overwhelming existential anguish which characterize the familial life. Mr. Abednego, the head of the family allows his unbridled sexual urge to push him into committing an incestuous crime. Rebecca the daughter of the home is so puerile and lackadaisical in her attitude towards serious issues. She is delighted to be acting in double capacity in the home. On the one hand, she is excited over her dual role in the home which motivates her to admonish her father to elope with her to an unknown destination as a means of escape from the wrath of her religiously ignorant mother. Mrs. Abednego, with a brooding sense of foreboding coupled with her exhibition of the traits of anticipatory grief, tells her son, that something very horrible was about to befall their household. On discovering the incestuous act, she becomes ballistic and apoplectic with rage; she murders her husband and daughter. She is arraigned for double homicide – a trial that may send her to a mad house, or the gallows.

Bozo becomes incapacitated with recent developments in his home. He is expelled from school for his bohemian lifestyle, especially his atheism. His home has crumbled and the world for him becomes a world of existential nausea, bleak, corrupt, deformed and lacking decency and security. As he becomes overwhelmed by his conditions, he experiences alienation through which he becomes isolated in a borderline mental condition. Although the crumbling of his home remains the activating event which provokes his experience of anarchistic depression, it is his mother's trial that provides him the actualizing tendency to traverse his solitude. He crosses the existential border-line through marijuana which he buys from Socrates. Bandele-Thomas' characters, especially Bozo, is not just divided through the unconscious or alienated by what Mary Lou Emery calls the "myth of the modern" (6), this loss of a natural self: they are fragmented most importantly through suppressed histories and eclipsed geo-cultural locations. Bozo, like Mensa, decides to alienate himself from this dark existential void where he lives and takes refuge in the woods and begins to cultivate marijuana. By this movement, he sustains himself within an alienating, adamic or, perhaps, edenic space-just like Friedrich Nietzsche's Zarathustra1. Bozo decides to flee his home, not because of any external agency but because of internally conflicted nature of the society and the contradiction with which it is riddled. Kanfanchan simply refuses to provide the consolation of home or, more appropriately, the consolation of the notion of home. Lewis Nkosi opines that "alienation, estrangement, an acute sense of anxiety are the immediate result of this lack of organic unity between the individual and the community..." (60). Bandele-Thomas achieves a double purpose with his narrative design. The fragmentation at the level of narration aptly reflects the psychological wrangling and mental dissonance of Bozo. The fragmentation at the level of narration is further complexified because of the multi-dimensionality of perspectives. Thus "Bandele-Thomas' novels reverberate with a real Babel of voices" (Okuyade "Teller" 523).

Although, the novel centres on Bozo's struggle with life or what he regards as the "system" (131), Lakemf remains the protagonist because he operates from the first narrative perspective and he bridges the hiatus between the reader and the world of the novel. Without his perspective the entire narrative will seem a romance tale; it therefore provides the entire story with credibility and through his perspective the novelist achieves realism. As the novel begins, the reader knows nothing of his past. We only meet him with other students ridiculing their literature teacher, Maude, because of his eccentricism. However his visit to the apartment of this eccentric teacher becomes the activating event which revolutionizes his entire life as a student and an individual trapped in a society that has gone awry because no body asks questions about moral and ethical issues. The novel employs the story telling motif to accentuate the importance of oral tale in Africa. Maude's manuscript is incomplete and the missing link has to be supplied to make the narrative whole. The story sessions actually begin with Maude's autobiography which he renders orally. The oral narrative is rendered with matter-of-factness and every incidence of this tale seems plausible. He narrates his ordeal with life as an orphan at a very tender age. The narrative captures the ignominious death of his mother which arrested his education in the bud. Unsatisfied with this oral tale that begins abruptly and disjointedly, Lakemf prodes further. The absence, excepting his mother, of other women in his tale is one point. To demonstrate he has had some degree of experience with women, Maude hands Lakemf the manuscript of his uncompleted novel which he eventually claims belongs to his brother. The reader and the protagonist meet another protagonist whose life begins to intercept with that of Lakemf.

Besides the fragmented narrative and the achronological plot structure, the novel aptly captures not just a society in transition, but an art form – a literature "in flux: it is a novel in transition moving from the oral mode to the written … towards the permanence of ink" (Okuyade "Beyond" 235). Oral tradition therefore, becomes the decimal that distinguishes African literature and the writer's authenticity of experiences and their collective identity. Critics and scholars have continued to place premium on socio-political issues when reading this novel, and most times lament the fragmentary nature of the novel. Jude Agho contends that "…many things are described so outlandishly that the novel looks disjointed in parts and the pace of narration reduced in the process" (42). The scatteredness of the novel, foregrounded in the narratological devices, does not only place the badge of orality on it, it is equally a signpost of textual interactions – the oral and the scribal. The irregular narration of the story through two different narrative modes – the oral, written and then oral only go to accentuate the importance of folklore to the African people and goes further to make bold the functionality of stories and the act of narrativisation. Besides the significance of orality which the narrative pattern articulates, the transitional narrative mode equally creates anxiety and suspense. This fact is aptly captured in the anxiety Lakemf expresses as the narrative gets broken at a point:

'So what happens next?' I asked. I was still ensconced in the raffia chair, a rained bottle of coke on the table before me. The guguru had disappeared and I had just finished the first part of Maude's uncompleted manuscript. I was not a little annoyed that he had chosen to break of at that particular point. (97)

Of the three books that provides textual mornings for this essay Bandele-Thomas' novel deals with a protagonist who does not die in the first couple of pages. The other two captures protagonists who die and are offered opportunity to review and edit their lives from the all-knowing vantage position. However, the protagonist in the third perspective of the narrative dies in page 25. It is until a couple of chapters later that we are furnished with details of his life and how he dies. Lakemf is afforded an opportunity to review himself and edit his activities as a student through the oral stories and the uncompleted manuscript of Maude's novel. He becomes overwhelmed by a character who becomes very revolutionary and insists he must change the system. Although, the system destroys him, the energy which he invests in the struggle is extraordinarily captivating. All attempts to talk him down fail. His resilience and unyielding temperament are what keep him alive in the woods for two years. He learns the act of survival alone and translates the pains of exile and the anguish of isolation into assets as he becomes an economic man. Bozo returns home like Daniel Defoe's Crusoe2, heavily beaded and unkempt but wiser making his story an interpretation as that of man's isolation and adjustment. However, after the sales of his products (Marijuana), he becomes moneyed and rather than do something tangible with his wealth he decides to rupture the system which he claims is responsible for the gross inequity in the society. Although his arrogance and smartness remain his biggest assets, it is his fearlessness and tactlessness that eventual destroy him.

Bozo invites his friends and adopts forty urchins (Almajiri) and begins his revolutionary strategy of redeeming the society from the hands of leaders who continue to mortgage the lives of the poor in the public sphere. His best friend, Socrates, dupes him. Rather than provide him grenades, he supplies him boxes filled with stones. His camp where he lodges his would be guerrilla-fighters is raided and his friends arrested for adoption. Frustrated by these developments, he raids the police station and murders every policeman on duty and commits suicide like Refentse, in order to avert the laws of the system.

Lakemf, becomes refined from these stories he has read and heard. He suddenly becomes transformed and his identity adjusted. He refuses to identify with his classmates in their nightly raid of the school poultry and the invasion of the school garden, stealing goats for a woman within the vicinity of the school, which she uses to prepare "pepper-soup" and the sales of science equipment stolen from the school science laboratory, ceiling fans and other items belonging to the school. He decides to tread the lonely path of revolutionaries. Lakemf's transformation, or metamorphosis, becomes complete as the narrative reaches denouement, because he does not only refuse to accompany Yau, his friend on their nightly rounds, he promises to confess his crimes before the principal and staff of the school regardless of the consequences of his actions: "I wanted a clean slate. To start from scratch. I wondered what my daddy's reaction would be when he heard of my confession." (40).

Regardless of the fact that Maude's tells Lakemf that the stories he has heard and read are all fictive, that the characters and incidences never existed, he still maintains his position to be transformed by these tales. His insistence on transforming his life provoked by the tales is a vibrant testimony to the didactic power of stories and the act of story telling. The first section of the story functions as an external quest for social identity and the concluding section functions as an internal quest for personal identity. The story of Bozo creates an awakening for Lakemf, through which he reassesses himself and discovers he is outside the central of morality. Although "the multiplication of fictional worlds, within the text makes it more fragmented and illogical coupled with numerous digression" (Okuyade "Modernist" 67), the act of story telling and the stories bequeath the novel with its uncompromising didactic tone and the eclecticism of folk culture and folk life.

These writers make the question of representation virtually important but frustratingly esoteric. This is so because of their narrative forms and modes which are deeply rooted in oral tradition. They seem to be writing beyond the ending,3 borrowing Duplessis expression, especially because they uncover the invisible and the indefinite. Besides the shifting form of the narrative designs of these texts and the adoption of spectra of orality, the narratives differ from other African texts of their generation in form. While most African narratives utilize traditional, linear, realistic form, these novels are highly fragmented, both in content and style. This fragmentation does not only represent the process through which the characters attempt to make sense of the illogicality of the world around them, but it accentuates the un-caulked lines which the collage of both the oral and the written forms engender, and the dialogical and dialectical relations between textualities. The conflation of realism with folk tradition creates a powerful dialogue between European and African literary traditions. These writers have extended the possibilities of other traditions. The writers have aptly demonstrated through narratology and multidimensionality of perspectives coupled with the oral slant noticed in the forms they have adopted that there is no clear-cut sense of realism in fiction. The narratives establish the fact that writers incorporate modernist and postmodernist insights into the creation of their arts, thereby fusing technical innovations with strong social concerns. By these formulas, they elaborate and extend the concept of realism in manifold directions. In acknowledging the functionality of linguistic codes and narrative forms in the articulation of meaning, the critic hardly dismisses the external world that literature engages, hence Andrze Gasiorek states that "out of this tension between the word and the world emerges a wide range of new realities" (183).

These three novels no doubt remain a difficult read, they challenge some of our cultural and aesthetic assumptions that we are not quite sure of what to make of them. They defy expectations of narrative structure and style, but they do not defy expectations of African literature considering the oral mode. Through these novels, these writers, especially Ce and Bandele-Thomas, open up new spaces for African writers and new spaces for the African identity, because besides performing the dual functions of literature: edutainment, they shock us out of our complacency and conformity and engage us with what must not be. They realize these assets by taking us back into the popular province of orature. Their narratives portray an enrichment of modern African literature especially fiction with regards to craft, demonstrating that the collaging of oral traditions with the modern mode of narrativisation could act as both creative innovation cum inspiration and artistic strategy in invigorating contemporary African fiction. They have artistically circumvented the Western notion of story telling in the novel genre by constructing a realism a little different from the Wattian popular construct of "formal realism". Although we may label Ce's form as spirito-mystic realism, or "complementary realism"4 , the fact remains that these writers have evolved and mapped alternative ways of representing the cultural consciousness rooted in their mythic imagination.

Chapter 6

The Mythic Context of Le Jujubier du patriarche

M. Guèye

IN the wake of the announcement of the death of grand narratives by postmodernism, postcolonial critics announced the death of such "essentialisms" as race, nation or even gender in their works.1 Aminata Sow Fall's Le Jujubier du patriarche2 illustrates that deconstructive vein of postcolonial literature with a discursive strategy, underwritten by the interaction of genres. Le Jujubier du patriarche opens in the mode of novelistic fiction and closes through that of epic poetry. Constructed in a dialogic relationship between the novel and the epic, the work transposes one genre, which is tied to the African oral tradition, into another, which emerges from the Western literary tradition.3 The novel's structure is characterized by the weaving of traditional mythological elements into a contemporary fictional text. This literary strategy allows the author to produce a narration written in the fiction of orality4 by creating a framework of oral enunciation via the technique of alternating voices. By achieving a collage of traditional speech within her novelistic discourse, Aminata Sow Fall makes Le Jujubier du patriarche emerge as the prolongation of the myth, which she installs at the core of the real.5 Here we examine the novelistic and epic styles of the work and the discursive implications that convey an ethno-nationalist counter-discourse on Senegalese society.

The novel opens with a narration that recounts the ritual pilgrimage to Babyselli that happens every year. The description of the physical setting lingers on a canal which used to be "the cradle of the Natangue6 river [...] [and] has long been dry, but [...] has had the time to crystallize, better to echo the epic song that tells the extraordinary adventures of their glorious ancestors" [le berceau du fleuve Natangué [...] [lequel] a tari depuis longtemps, mais [...] a eu le temps de se cristalliser pour mieux rendre l'écho du chant épique qui conte les aventures extraordinaires de leurs glorieux ancêtres] (9). In combining the past of such a locus with the present of the residents and pilgrims that inhabit it, the novel's opening announces, through the temporal interlacing of the narration, the interaction of genres that dominates the work's structure. Due to this dialogic composition, Le Jujubier du patriarche stands as a work that narrates a dramatic present against a heroic past. According to Goldenstein, narrative opening signals involve an actual reading pact often based on a fully codified rhetoric of fictional beginnings.7

A symptomatic adulteration is behind the logic of the story in Le Jujubier du patriarche, which resembles a chronicle of individual and community dysfunction. The novel recounts the hardship of Yelli's noble family trying to find a salvaging equilibrium in an environment of "moral decrepitude where the human no longer meant anything" [décrépitude morale où l'humain n'avait plus de sens] (63). From this perspective, the work depicts the failure of the individual to harmoniously integrate into society, and the quest for communal meaning lost in a rampant, unbridled modernity. It is the representation of a societal alienation that tellingly resembles the context that engendered the novel in the Western world. Indeed the novel translates the divorce between the individual and the world, and makes reference to a societal alienation as discussed in Lukàcs' Hegelian hypothesis on the unity of the ancient world: "The novel is the result of the epic's decay.8" [Le roman est le résultat de la décomposition de l'épique]. This commentary echoes Bernstein's in The Philosophy of the Novel: "If the hallmark of the epic is its subjectlessness, then it might be argued that subjectivity as such is what makes modernity problematic."9 The rift between the social and the individual and its pernicious consequences violate the norms of traditional ethic in Le Jujubier du patriarche. Read from this angle, the novel joins other works by Aminata Sow Fall in depicting an alienated community where the search for authentic values is presented as the ultimate solution to societal dysfunction.

Thus, Le Jujubier du partriarche, following the modern novel, tells stories.10 However, its narrative unity is inherent in the plot despite the interaction of genres, which characterizes the composition. This plot articulates the pilgrimage of a dislocated family to Babyselli, a mythical city, in order to listen to the epic and rebuild the symbolic universe of the group identity.11 As George

Ngal asserts, the plot "is the synthesis of that which is disparate in the novel"12 [est la synthèse de ce qui dans le roman est hétéroclite]. The distinct narrative makeup in Le Jujubier du patriarche is the ensemble of various actions whose organization reveals a macrostructure that generally corresponds with the classical dramatic structure of exposition, climax, and denouement: The description of Yelli's dramatic situation (exposition), the reaction of his wife, Tacko,13 to this situation and its consequences on the decision of their adopted daughter, Naarou, to revive the epic (climax), and finally the pilgrimage to Babyselli, where the epic of Foudjallon will be sung (denouement).14

Le Jujubier du patriarche narrates simultaneously - in novelistic terms - the prosaism of urban life at the "end of the twentieth century" [fin du vingtième siècle] (12) led by Yelli and his family and – in epic terms – the heroism of an era that extends across "seven hundred years of the history of the Almamy line and that of the hunters of Foudjallon" [sept cents ans d'histoire de la lignée des Almamy et de celle des chasseurs du Foudjallon] (14-15). It is this epic story of one hundred and ten thousand lines that the epic mode of Le Jujubier du patriarche illustrates, using a mise en abyme of orality. This narrative technique allows the author to insert into the primary narrator's discourse, which makes reference to the epic, the voice of the character who sings that very epic. This strategy -providing, sometimes quite explicitly, sometimes more allusively, a framework for enunciation that brings the narrator face to face with the auditor of the story- is clearly an excellent pre-text for oralizing discourse.15

By transposing the oral performance into Le Jujubier du patriarche, the author produces a story within the story through two narrative strategies that alternate in creating a context of oral enunciation. (A-) The primary narrator reports the action of the epic and notes that the traditional narrative voice is telling this story to an audience. This procedure begins systematically with an introductory sentence that alludes to the epic tale being reported. In the text, it is distinguished from the second process, which is in the form of verse, by its prose style. Due to this indirect strategy, the author confers onto the primary narrator the status of traditional narrative voice and finds, in addition, a way to summarize the long epic song by performing a selective narration, which privileges the relevant genealogy of Yelli's family. (B-) The second narrative strategy involves replacing the primary narrator with the traditional narrator: The framework of enunciation is given as an oral performance, a context of communication in which there is interaction between the traditional narrator (griot) and his audience; all these roles are played by characters identifiable in the novelistic story. Le Jujubier du patriarche illustrates this process through the griot Naani, reciting one episode in the epic, and through Naarou, reciting another. Through these processes of oral production replicated in Le Jujubier du patriarche, Aminata Sow Fall moves into an "anatomy lesson" of the Sudano-Sahelian epic by respecting the modalities of the genre's formation.16

The epic of Foudjallon is a narration of origins and its role in Le Jujubier du patriarche is double: "The objectives of Naarou and Yelli were not of the same sort, of course..." [L'objectif de Naarou et de Yelli n'était pas du même genre, bien sûr…] (92). On one hand, the song of the illustrious ancestors represents a nostalgic return to the glorious past for Yelli and for the community assembled at Babyselli.17 On the other hand, and from the point of view of Naarou, it is the pretext for a subversion of the grand narrative,18 which marginalizes her slave ancestors, such as Sadaga and Biti, to whom the song should also pay homage because of their link to the dynastic clan and their heroic service to it.

From Yelli's perspective, the pilgrimage to Babyselli allowed the entire community to see and to realize that "myths are still accessible" [les mythes sont encore accessibles] (91). These myths, through the strength of their evocation, have the power to rejuvenate lost hopes, as suggested by the parable of the jujube tree in the novel.19

For Naarou, the song of the forebearers carries a more complex signification. It holds the same cultural function as for Yelli and the other members of the community assembled at Babyselli. However, to Naarou there is much more than the mere fact of feeling exultation: "To see that myths are accessible, but no longer simply through the ecstatic pleasure kindled through their evocation" [Voir que les mythes sont accessibles non plus seulement par le plaisir extatique que leur évocation suscite] (91). Indeed, Naarou is interested in the perception of renewed identity, cultural and ideological, projected through the text of the epic of Foudjallon. She is well aware of this ideological accentuation, which hardly privileges her identity as a griot because she has always had a particular interest in the epic and its recitation.

When, as a young girl, Naarou decided to understand the mechanisms in the creation of an epic, she promised herself to deconstruct this grand narrative in order to include the narration of her own origins, since the heroism of the Almamy could not have happened without her slave forebearers: "I descend from the line of Warèle and Biti, who played a key role in the epic. [...] Who said they were not of royal blood" [Je descends de Warèle et de Biti qui ont joué un rôle déterminant dans l'épopée. [...] Qui dit qu'elles n'étaient pas de sang royal] (69). It is evident that Naarou's words can find a parallel in the debate around the narratological confusion between history and fiction as modes of discourse.

Since the epic is frequently defined as a genre situated between history and myth – in other words, between reality and imagination – Naarou knows, as does the oral narrator in Kourouma's Monnè, that the griot has the power to make the world by naming it, to construct the past and invent the future, to create the official story and the historical truth imposed by it.20 For that reason, taking advantage of a funeral ceremony organized at the death of Yelli's father, she composes a song "in order to integrate it into the chapter about Wally" [pour l'intégrer au chapitre de Wally] (73) and proudly recites it before the public, thus revealing the familial link that ties her family to Yelli's and Tacko's, and consequently ties it to the princely aristocracy of Foudjallon. Naarou's appropriation of the official text is underwritten by her mastery of narratological rules as well as by the cultural and ideological function of the traditional epic tale.21

Thus, if Yelli and the community assembled at Babyselli are primarily motivated by the cultural function of the epic in Le Jujubier du patriarche, Naarou is conversely motivated by its ideological function, which she exploits for her own benefit. Indeed, if the history of her ancestors had been censured from the epic of Foudjallon, it is because "the practice never considered preserving the genealogy of slaves" [l'usage ne prévoyait pas de retenir la généalogie des esclaves] (29-30).

As stated by Case, the aesthetic of the text can only be revealed through a comprehension of its use of different genres, each bringing some specific meaning to the structure and symbolism of the novel.22 This is so in Le Jujubier du patriarche, for through the interaction of the novelistic and epic forms, which characterizes the novel's structure, Aminata Sow Fall produces an ethno-nationalist discourse on Senegalese society.

In the symbolism of Le Jujubier du patriarche, the discursive intention of Aminata Sow Fall can be read as a celebration of the process of encounter, of symbiosis, as a sort of universal remedy against the societal evils that plague postcolonial Africa. So it is evident that while the epic of Foudjallon is set in an ethnic space specific to the Peuls,23 it gathers together the cultural elements of all the large ethnic groups of the sub-region. It then emerges as a site of synthesis and revitalization of mythic and epic motifs and schemas of the West Sahelian zone.24 The release announcing the pilgrimage to Babyselli makes it clear that it is a trans-ethnic event which presides over the recitation of the epic of Foudjallon: "A press release was printed in the newspaper, in which the descendents of Almamy Sarebibi invited the entire community, without distinction to sex, ethnicity or religion, to the pilgrimage to Babyselli" [Un communiqué de presse parut dans le journal, par lequel les descendants de l'Almamy Sarebibi conviaient toute la communauté sans distinction de sexe, d'ethnie ou de religion, au pèlerinage à Babyselli] (92). Le Jujubier du patriarche can therefore be linked to Toucouleur (Peul) and Wolof cultural foundations respectively. It is a symbiotic move that is at the heart of Aminata Sow Fall's discourse in the novel, and it is manifest likewise through Naarou's subversion since the return to tradition assumes an ideological [de]-construction that is marked by current realities.25 This emblematic synthesis is also found in several layers of the text of Le Jujubier du patriarche. It can be read in the figure of the epic hero Yellimané who embodies, through his tireless striving, the myth of Sisyphus26 in his attempt to reunite the rival clans in the ancestral epic. And he himself is the symbol of this union: "'He is of his father and of his mother' had recognized both parts. Half from the moon to learn the art of the hunt, half to prepare himself to be the worthy son of l'Almamy... " ['Il est de son père et de sa mère' avaient reconnu les deux parties. Moitié de lune pour apprendre l'art de la chasse, moitié pour s'entraîner à être le digne fils de l'Almamy...] (102). So the epic of Foudjallon implicitly lauds this métissage, and the choice of such a symbolic language speaks about the hybrid character of Senegalese society, which the author wants to reaffirm: "Man gets his strength and his resistance from alliance" [L'homme tire sa force et sa résistance des alliages] (119). Through Le Jujubier du patriarche, Aminata Sow Fall critiques the value system, based on a social hierarchy, that placed the géér at the summit of Senegalese society because of ancestry instead of merit. This position questions the essentialism, fed by

131

a caste sensibility, which underlies societal inequalities, and proposes a vision of identity that is in keeping with métissage, whether it be that of ethnicity or of caste, and which represents the true paradigm of Senegalese society.

The essence of Le Jujubier du patriarche resides in the interaction of the novelistic and the epic forms. Its literary métissage symbolizes the texture of the social melting pot of Senegal and allows the work to be read as a palimpsest text that advocates multiculturalism. Intertextuality functions symbolically in this work to signify social polyphony. This is achieved by incorporating echoes of the multiple channels that make up Senegalese society into the polyphony that is formed by the combination of the voices of characters such as Naani, Naarou, and the griots who continue to recite epics from Foudjallon to Babyselli, as they have done in the past. In view of the author's revival of traditional aesthetics, her combination of multiple genres and cultural elements, and Naarou's perception of the epic as socially constructed, we could say that in Le Jujubier du patriarche, Aminata Sow Fall also wins a difficult wager in making a postmodern epistemology work in a Sahelian mythic context.27

Le Jujubier du patriarche continues the discourse on identity of L'Appel des arènes by depicting the same binary thematic between the present and the past. Where Ndiattou exaggerates the value, more significant in her eyes, of modernity and Western culture in L'Appel des arènes, in Le Jujubier du patriarche, through her shocking behavior with Naarou, Tacko introduces the same theme by inflating her aristocratic lineage, sustained through the manipulation of oral tradition. This structure of opposition in the service of the discourse on identity is part of the aesthetics of fiction for Aminata Sow Fall, who believes that human beings will find salvation through equilibrium, and through the ability to assimilate all influences, to blend the past and the present, so as to move towards the future.

Chapter 7

Oral Performance among the Graffi

D Neba Che

THE term Grasslanders or what has been called 'Grassland fielders', also known in Cameroon English as Graffi (Nkwi 11) dates back to German colonial times. Germany, one of the colonizers of Cameroon, used it to designate that part of the hinterlands characterized by high altitude and extensive flora. Quoting Danker, Nkwi says it is the "sea of grass which stretches for hundreds of kilometers providing one of the most magnificent panoramas on earth". And in portraying this topography he adds that "except for the forest galleries, early travelers to the region were usually impressed by the beautiful grassy landscape" (11).

The above nomenclature initially had a geographical bearing but further ethnographic studies have proven that Graffi or 'Grassland' or 'Grass fields' as used within the Cameroon context also has anthropological and cultural signification. The culture of the Graffi is, in a nutshell, that of the Tikar. Grasslanders are spread over at least five of the ten regions of Cameroon: North West, South West, Centre, West and Adamawa (Banyo) regions.

'Grassland' as used here incorporates the cultural similarities that are identifiable among this people.

The role of performers in the numerous and linguistically diverse ethnic groups throughout the Grasslands of the North West Region of Cameroon is basically the same, and although some slight differences exist, they only help to distinguish performers from each other. Even when the songs or the tales of the Graffi are not the same, the manner of actualizing them and the themes they treat are fundamentally the same. Each performer tries to preserve the culture of the people. Consequently, in each performance, performers strive to display their artistic ingenuity in order to establish their identity. In addressing the performer as preserved tradition and original creator, we redefine the role of the performer and bring out his role in oral performances.

The performer projects a dual identity: as tradition and as creator. As tradition he has two functions. He serves as a cultural reservoir because he is capable of performing expected texts within defined contexts. He knows exactly what to do, how to do it, when to do it and what his audience expects of him. Besides the general tradition of the people he also respects the tradition of the text. In short, he incarnates the people's culture. Besides being the embodiment of the Graffi tradition, he is also a creator. Through his creative talent, new texts are produced in each performance – giving no room for a repetitive exercises. The performer therefore gives life to oral performances. Since the life of the text is in the hands of the performer, he can be seen as the nucleus of traditional literature.

From a scientific perspective , the nucleus controls all metabolic activities in the cell. Its shape varies from species to species and from tissue to tissue. Above all, it is the most important organelle in the cell. If an oral performance is likened to the cell, it therefore comes round to truth that the performer automatically plays the role of the nucleus in the cell. Without the nucleus the cell is non-living. Thus there is no orature without performers.

The activity of the performers of folksongs or oral narratives among the Graffi of the North West Region of Cameroon varies from one context to another depending on the temperament or mood of the performer. This flexibility in oral performances gives the performer the impetus to create and re-create during performances. Being a custodian of culture, he makes little or no effort to break 'traditionally' passed-on phrases and incidence; as a result, his work is to render performances more lively and spontaneous.

The Case of Performance as Tradition

The performer as tradition is seen in two folds: tradition of the text and that of the society which combine to give the tradition of the people in general. Examining the performer as an embodiment of the people's tradition, Mateso states:

S'inscrivant en faux contre une conception qui ne veut voir dans l'artiste qu'un robot au service de la communauté, (...) la "littérarité' de soumission, de liberté de fidélité dont fait montre le conteur ou le barde

dans la transmission de l'héritage ancestral. Loin
d'être le fruit d'une concentration des determinismes,
l'œuvre orale comporte une intentionalité conciente, celle
de l'artiste restructurant activement le 'vaste texte virtuel
et objectif de tradition.' (29-30)

Reiterating the role of the performer as tradition,
Mateso further opines:

L'intervention de l'artiste consiste donc en une
actualisation de la tradition (relecture), celle-ci comporte
néccessairement une   critique. Il n'y a donc pas de
difference irréductible entre l'œuvre et sa critique.
L'observateur de la tradition peur trouver cette
conception de la critique qui a survécu dans le theater
moderne.(30)

Interestingly, the performer safeguards the tradition of
the people by preserving and transmitting the message of
the ancestors. As with the Graffi of the North West
Region before mounting the podium, performers remind
the audience of certain things that the ancestor said or
show how they were taught to execute certain actions like
ritual incantations. One informant in a bid to show his
importance as the custodian of the people's culture and
his awareness for preserving it, claimed that 'there are no
two people in this village who can narrate this story the
way I am doing. Go out and search.''1 Firstly, he asserts
himself as the lone archive in existence. Secondly, he is
the lone person who knows the tradition of the text in
terms of respecting form, content and narrative
technique. Finally, the pride he displays in his art intends

to prove that nobody can manage the audience the way he does. These assertions, although somehow exaggerated, go a long way in ascertaining the position of the performer among the Graffi people as the custodian of the people's culture and tradition.

The Abinimfor festival in Nkwen and Bafut,2 the Lela festival among the Bali Nyonga,3 Njang in Akum,4 the Mbaghalum among the Bafouchu, Nkwen and Mankon5 and dirge performances are all occasions during which performers respect both the tradition of the people and that of the text. From all indications, the performances of the Abinimfor and Lela festivals and other oral performances are perfect domains of iconic and indexical significations. The performer in Graffi knows the exact costume of his social status in the society and consequently knows the type of 'tughe'6 to wear. In the performances, the relationship between the signifier and the signified is apparent and casual.

The costume worn by the performer indicates the different social classes within the Grassfield. For example, titleholders wear the 'nitong'.7 The quality of the costume and the decoration reinforces the idea of class stratification in the Graffi. Since the Abinimfor in Bafut, Nkwen and Mankon are royal performances, the royal family and title holders distinguish themselves by putting on high quality costumes. Their social status is portrayed in their dress. In the Abinimfor in Bafut, the different titles worn by the performers range from the red feather to the porcupine's stick, and finally the bag with rings for men and the 'bow',8 for women. In the Lela festival, the Bali people have their own method of using costumes and props to distinguish and identify performers. For example military leaders are identified by their costumes. It is therefore expedient to note that the Bali people are not as bellicose as was the case before and during German colonization of Cameroon. Today, warlords are people who bring fortune of any kind into the village. Those who serve as plenipotentiaries of the Bali Kingdom are often honoured with titles during the Lela festival. During performances, their regalia and hand props speak. Thus costume and the props are iconising or are indexically significant.

Looking at the actor-character relationship, the masquerade performer loses his identity in Njang songs and becomes something else in his Njang costume. Most often, he represents the society's view of the particular mask he is carrying. For example, he might be carrying the mask of a lion, which signifies bravery and power. It might be the mark of an owl representing ill omen or plaque. The various stage props like tiger skins, carved images, paintings on walls, elephant tusks, cutlasses, spears and other cultural elements displayed during performances either associate (indexically) or substitute (iconically) something in the people's culture. For example, the tiger skin and elephant tusk are associated with bravery and leadership; the carved images and most paintings are icons of past glories. Symbols of village totems, the brandishing of cutlasses and spears, associated with heroism and war are brought to life by the performer who is the nucleus and catalyst of the story.

Another important aspect to note is that during these festivals (particularly the Abinimfor), performers dance in lines and each line is made up of people of particular social status. Other performers know when the village king or chief is coming in to perform, and what they are expected to do. The king or chief comes into the performance circle in a royal way (most often with distinguished regalia) and dances in a royal manner, which consists of gun salutations and clapping from other performers and audience. Some performers during the Abinimfor welcome his entrance with a change of the rhythm of the orchestra and with ululations. The court jesters respect the tradition of keeping the audience awake by forcing chewed corn into the mouths of those who seem carried away by the performance or who are absent minded. Each performer knows what tradition demands of him. Since the performer is the embodiment of the people's tradition, he tries as much as he can to be perfect and honest in his performance. Helen Chukwuma comments that 'the traditional artist is thus every/man and any man and woman sufficiently knowledgeable in the literary traditions of the people and capable of communicating this in an entertaining way to an audience... the traditional activist is a cultural transmitter' (226). His intention is usually fidelity in performance. In respecting his art therefore, the performer in turn respects the tradition of the people.

The medium through which societal symbols, values, history, religious beliefs, morals and social relationships are stored and propagated to the people's satisfaction is the performer whose importance in society increases as the society constantly turns to them as references. In order to maintain continuity, especially in the performance of songs and dance, lead singers or good performers are always rewarded with money. This encourages young performers to learn the arts as they grow. Some accompany their parents to all occasions as a means of initiating themselves into the art. In order to encourage them, a small circle for children is usually formed in the middle of bigger circles in Njang performances in Akum and Bafut. Since those who have mastered the art are choreographers in performance, the children in their own way imitate and eventually come out of the inner circle as they grow. This also occurs in the performance of the Abinimfor and Lela festival dances/songs.

The narrators of oral narrative among the Graffi also attach importance both to the tradition of the text and that of the people as they are able to decipher when and how to narrate legends, myths and folklores. Legend and myth narrators are often seen as living archives. The past annals of the village are with them. They come out on special occasions to let the younger generation know more about the society in which they find themselves. As cultural reservoirs, they master the narrative techniques of these oral narratives. They know how to introduce and end stories. Sometimes very important narrations are introduced with a riddle game that touches on the main theme. Albert B. Lord has noted that this "art consists not so much in learning through repetition of the timeworn formulas as in the ability to compose and recompose the phrases for the idea of the moment on the pattern established by the basic formulas" and concludes that "He is not a conscious iconoclast, but a traditional creative artist" (5).

Some of the dances—the Lela festival song/dance and the Abinimfor festival song/dance in addition to the

141

Njang, Mansoh9 Mbaghalum and most masquerade dances are accompanied by a special orchestra. Performers with little or no training, but who respect the tradition, dance systematically. In the actualization of Mbaghalum songs, performers pair themselves in groups, dance systematically into the circle, break the turns into quarters, towards the left, most often in a 'u' form, move back to their original position and give way to other pairs. Masquerade dancers are also more choreographic than other dance groups because they go into many practice sessions before performances. In most of these choreographic performances, the role of the lead singer, who is also the chief choreographer, is very instrumental. Since he masters the tradition of the people and that of the texts in particular, he is capable of directing other performers with much ease and making performances colourful. Some of the performers are familiar with the tradition of the text in such a way that sometimes just a broad smile or the lifting of hands can give a new pace to the performance.

Having examined the central role of the lead performers in African performances, Ziky Kofoworola and Yusef Lateef note that "the choreography is rightly the producer in performances based on music, dance and mime art from an age-old tradition" arguing that

from the point of view of the African tradition the choreographer in the sense of the man who organizes a dance event is considered as the producer of the performance. In African situations, such persons usually take part in the leading role of a dance performance as well as making sure that the dance steps and movements of other dancers are in accordance with the designed patterns synchronized with the rhythm of the music. (165)

Thus these choreographers serving as custodians of the tradition of the text are also creators since they give life to performances.

The Case of Performance as Creation

Albert Lord in his own examination of the creative role of the performer had upheld that "his style …has individuality, and it is possible to distinguish the songs of one singer from those of another, even when we have only the bare song without music and vocal nuance" (5). Expanding on the concept of creativity in orature, Rosenberg makes an important point: "Writing" he states, "does something 'unnatural' to the life of an authentic oral lyric or narrative";

it concretizes it, removes it from the living stream of its existence. For one thing, literature in print deprives the performer of all the histrionic skills of performance, while it also proscribes the possibility of change in the text, as an oral reciter might well make minor adjustment in his or her material depending on his or her inclinations and those of the audience. An older woman, for instance, might tell a certain tale involving a sexual encounter one way to her friends, another way to the village priest and still quite another to her grandchild. (93)

It is therefore evident that an oral performance is interplay between creativity and cultural expectations. The assertion of an identity in each performance by performers and their manipulation of local norms and lore become essential factors in understanding performances. As each performer asserts his identity through his artistic ingenuity, the result is a new text. We find that oral performers freely manipulate language, content and context to a desired effect. What often retains the audience especially, in the performances of songs among the Graffi, is the performer's ability to create. In most of the Njang songs, whose content is mostly satirical, it suffices for the lead singer to throw his eyes on somebody and immediately use the person's name for comments on his character. The performer's ability to chain up songs of the same rhythm makes the performance more interesting and helps the audience to play its dual role of performers and audience. As Jack Mapanje and Landeg White state:

When the song was well sung everybody admired. When it was badly sung, everybody knew it. If the language was fresh, the singer was praised for his imagination. If the song was simply repeated without new insight it was rejected. (4)

What, therefore, keeps the audience alive in oral performances is the performer's ability to be creative through the use of fresh language, a strong voice, retentive memory, and the use of paralinguistic and kinesic features to captivate the audience. In short, he must be able to whet the appetite of his judges. As such, "in approaches to performance as something creative, the character of the narrator comes into play–the language, how the lines are arranged, the metaphors, similes, paralinguistic resources such as nods, exclamations, facial expressions..." (Okerere 41). This character intrusion through the performer's artistic creativity is what gives him authorship, and consequently makes him a creator in each performance.

In the myth of a beautiful princess who got married and traveled to the land of the dead, a Graffi narrator from Nkwen describes the heroine as having 'dancing breasts'. Dancing breasts here is opposed to shrunken breasts. To let the audience understand him well he had to create a visual image of erect breasts by describing them metaphorically as dancing. In any case, he reminds his audience that dancing does not refer to the conscious art of dancing but rather to the motion of her breasts as she walks. This ability of each performer to exploit the linguistic, paralinguistic and kinesic resources to communicate his message depends on individual talents. As indicated earlier, the way a performer will narrate a myth or a legend to an audience made up of elders where he sums up many things in proverbial expressions is not the way he will narrate it to a mixed audience.

The creative ability of the performer in Graffi land also depends on how he manages the constituents of the paradigmatic and the syntagmatic axes of the text and beyond. His ability to substitute words so as to create vivid imagery or to associate them adds a flare to the performance which can never be realized in writing. The problem is not narrating a tale or singing a song to the public, but knowing how to exploit the linguistic and the paralinguistic resources at his disposal. The success of each oral rendition therefore depends on the performer's ability to create. Improvisation becomes one of the main tools of creation. Performers in orature are quick to exploit the circumstances that surround each performance: visual and auditory images and other images that pertain to the rest of our senses.

A successful exploitation of these resources by performers keeps the audience at ease and establishes a sense of harmony between parties. When there is a liaison between the performer and audience, the result is cognitive satisfaction where both groups are able to relate individual images raised to a theme or comment on certain aspects of human behavior in the community. For this cognitive satisfaction to be attained the performer must be able to respond to stimuli in all circumstances. He needs not spare any opportunity which can help him to successfully transmit his message and keep his audience for a whole night with a captivating and talented rendition of a story or song which, though it might be familiar, is articulated with a creative avalanche of paralinguistic and even kinesic elements borrowed from the performer's ingenuous repertoire. Because he struggles to set a good pace for his audience, each performance becomes a new experience and a very unique adventure.

In conclusion what gives life or existence to any oral text is the performer. A videocassette repeatedly played presents the same author with stagnant images and no traces of creativity. The linguistic, paralinguistic or kinesic features will be the same, even if the cassette were played a million times. However, it is the lesser evil, since many do not want to analyze during performance. Scholars of orature should be able to carry out all analyses in performance and to do so repeatedly if their objective is to grasp the realities of oral performances. Since the death of the performer may equally be that of the text, printed or video performances should be attempts to reach the public with the carcass of the oral text. The central role that a nucleus plays in an atom or in a cell is the same role that the performer plays in oral performances. As the context changes, the style of performance also changes. There is no way we can talk of orature without first focusing on the performer. For "the traditional artist is a modeler of tradition and can be said to be 'creative' only in the fact of giving a good and full rendering of materials he had already learned" (Chukwuma 227).

Conclusion

Critical attempts at treating oral texts out of performance have yielded little fruit, showing that nothing can effectively replace live performance. In order to store this rich cultural heritage, new bards, soloists and dancers should be trained in life performances. It is a challenge for Africans and lovers of its culture to maintain this creative method of transmitting the people's culture. The presence of the performer is a living proof of the survival of the people's tradition. It is therefore important that a piece of oral literature be analysed in performance. It is only through this medium that the role of the performer can clearly be seen as an embodiment of creation and tradition. In the efforts within critical circles to attain a faithful record on transcribing and translating an oral text, may only just be struggling to give a seeming picture of the real oral text to those who depend on written or recorded material for analyses.

Chat

Chapter 8

Sembene: Last Chat with an African Griot

[This discussion was held in Dakar, Senegal, shortly before Ousmane's death in June 2007.]

J E. Obitaba

OB: Who is a beggar?

SE: Is it not the one who begs?

OB: That sounds to me like a sweeping statement.

SE: Yes. As a researcher, you should know it is the one who begs.

OB: So anyone who stretches an arm to receive a favour is called a beggar.

SE: Yes, several times, if one does it every day, at the corner of the street (in the offices) ... yes, one is a beggar.

OB: If I understand you well, it is hereby implied that standing at a corner and stretching an arm to receive alms constitutes begging. Isn't this...?

SE: Yes, of course. That, we can classify as begging. There is this other category too: There are now the corrupt people inside the offices in the administration (and) also corrupt police officers who stand at the corners of the roads.

OB: So the clerks, officers, the orderlies, the guards in our ministries who are always broke before the end of the month, all these people can be called "beggars?"

SE: One cannot say flat out they are beggars, but when they use their offices for corruption, there are nevertheless beggars, if you want. Like the one who sits at the corner of the streets or in front of the mosque… to that we can agree. Now there are countries in Africa such as Nigeria or Senegal where one sees the petty civil servant who does not manage to tie both ends (before the end of the month) becoming corrupt… people like that we can accept as belonging to a rotten system of beggars.

OB: And the unemployed of various categories who trudge our roads?

SE: They will end up being beggars. Look at your cities in Nigeria: Kano, Maiduguri….

OB: (And cities in) Burkina-Faso, Mali too.

SE: Yes, look at the number of people who become insane… the young people starting from 30 to 40 years of age. That is due to unemployment, lack of work, eh…? It is so serious that they are ready to beg. We know of these fathers or mothers in the streets of Dakar on Friday… It is no more a secret you see… there are women who have twins, who have two children, who beg.

OB: But for the women who have twins, there seems to be one reason. For example, at the Aiyetoro, a Yoruba community in Nigeria, there are these women who beg, and they do that because it is a rite, i.e. begging became for them…

SE: Wait. I do not know how that is done in Nigeria. Here in traditional community of Wolof, this begging by the mothers of twins was done only one day per week and for one hour at that. Moreover, the twins should be no more than seven years old.

OB: That is to say that begging was done like a rite too.

SE: It is like a rite. That is, done one day per week and from one certain hour defined in the places given. Now if you look at, well, instead of going to the mosque people band themselves around traffic lights.... Yes, they flock around red lights. I do not know if you already read *The Last of the Empire*?

OB: No, not yet.

SE: There is where you will see the description

OB: If I grasp very well what you are saying, people exploit the ritual ceremony of begging in Senegal.

SE: Yes.

OB: Can one call somebody who renders a simple service "a beggar" because the service is not orthodox?

SE: No, because it is not a stupid trade.

OB: Can one call the Third World countries which lick the bottom of the International Monetary Fund (I. M. F) and the World Bank (to have loans) beggars? How do you characterize these countries?

SE: You see, for development, it is not begging. One can say that for development, a country needs investments. Are you in agreement?

OB: Yes, yes.

SE: Therefore these countries move to go to seek capital to develop such or such sectors of their economy.

OB: According to what you have just said, it seems to me that there is a condition of begging implicit in the actions of these countries.

SE: No, that is not the picture we are given. It is us who suppose that when African Heads of States move to seek investment, we say they went to beg.

OB: So in the true sense of the word, they are not beggars. Even if it means that these negotiations with the I. M. F and World Bank end only in misery.

SE: Yes, let it be known that when our Heads of State leave abroad to seek capital and they return with money, we, Senegalese and Nigerians, say in bad faith that our Heads of State went to beg because the word "to beg" is anchored in our head. Do you understand?

OB: Yes, yes.

SE: It is a popular word because the beggar who is, from the social point of view, down the bottom begs and the Head of State "begs" also, but the two actions differ.

OB: That's it?

SE: The two points differ; that is what I want to say to you.

OB: Please what are the causes of begging?

SE: It is difficult to say what the precise causes of begging are. One can say that it is poverty because people are deprived. Ok? It is what one can say. That is one apparent cause: one is poor and deprived. In addition, there is no desire to honour the religious injunctions on the act.

OB: Good! Where does begging originate? I mean.... In human beginnings there were no beggars. Even in feudal times, begging assumed a different character from what it is today. And how is independence responsible for begging?

SE: I did not say that. I did not say that.

OB: And the dryness and famine?

SE: Good. Those are factors.... It is not independence; economic and ecological factors cause that. Let us take for example England a hundred years ago at the beginning of industrialization.... Or France. In England we have the book of Camus (Albert) *The Outsider* and we have in France, the book of Hugo (Victor) *The Poor Wretches*. You see, it is not independence at all. There are economic factors and one can go around on a world tour to see.

OB: If I understand you well, the famine destroyed all and the ground does not yield any more....

SE: Yes, you can say that is an ecological factor, and it is not only that; the famine perhaps accentuated, worsened it. The destitution of people, of the peasants, is so much that they leave, that they give up the ground for the city. However they do not have there an exact trade anymore and they depend on community or religious solidarity to beg.

OB: What Marxist interpretation can you give to the phenomenon of begging?

SE: That a capitalist system protects the rich minority and, by this objective, it goes without saying that beggars emerge because the great majority does not have much to consume; it can never benefit from the system where there is no right and equitable distribution of the means production.

OB: So why did you write *Xala*, your famous work?

SE: It was a fight known in Senegalese community as hélée. *Xala* does not speak about the origin of the beggars.... With the middle-class becoming increasingly small, begging -the beggars- grew increasingly numerous. But *Xala* is a kind of metaphor.

OB: Do you think that *Xala* is a better work compared to the *Ambiguous Adventure* from this thematic point of view?

SE: That I should not say.... That is for literary criticism to say.

OB: Can you indicate, either in precise or general way, the manpower of the workers in Senegal in 1960 or the eighties?

SE: That don't I know... the manpower of the workers?

OB: Yes.

SE: Workers?

OB: Yes.

SE: The manpower of the workers, the civil servant and the peasants?

OB: Yes, either in 1960 or at beginning of the 80s.

SE: That I do not know. There must have been statistics.... I know that there were censuses which checked manpower, the exact number of the workers, the workers of factories, the civil servants but I did not really have the exact figures.

OB: In general, there was an imbalance in the manpower of the workers (workmen included)?

SE: I do not know what you want to say or what your objective is. If you asked me how the reports/ratios are done, that is another thing. There are workmen who work without having even factories; there are civil servants. There are workmen; there are tradesmen. You understand what I want to say?

OB: Yes, yes.

SE: And that poses problems. Compared to the peasants, we are placed better. The peasants currently work only three or four months in the year. That is the practice. Good....

OB: Why such a short work period?

SE: You see, we have just spoken about the famine at the beginning of our discussion. It is that.

OB: Do you believe that the beggars play a useful part in the society?

SE: What (do you mean by) "to play"?

OB: Yes, you believe that the beggars play...

SE: Yes, I understand, but play how?

OB: Do you believe that a beggar plays a useful part?

SE: Yes, of course, but play how? Does a beggar play an exemplary part? I can ask you this question and it is important to answer me. Is it a role... a role in the society to forget to bring something to the society? If one is a consumer only, what role can one play?

OB: Like the prayer, the blessing which the beggars do offer to people who need them, can one regard them as service or production?

SE: No, one cannot regard them as production. Moreover, it is necessary to distinguish the standards, the ethics of life, between the two classes. Between the two, one gives and the other receives. Yes. It is important to see the two are not within the same framework.

OB: What are your own judgments?

SE: I do not have judgments. I do not have judgments. I know that a society can become beggars but that of the capitalist system can only populate more beggars.

OB: The religions, i.e., Islam and Christianity, approve that disabled persons who are not able to provide for their own needs can beg, but your beggar who is crippled does not accept his state to be that of a beggar, why?

SE: But listen, it is necessary to leave a fixed and personal premise nevertheless. No father, no, mother would like his/her children to become beggars. It is necessary to start from there. It is precisely that which creates problem in the heart of a mother. Every father or mother wishes that his/her son or daughter becomes someone in life. Do you understand me?

OB: Yes.

SE: But here is the problem. In countries where there have been transitions and revolutionary upheavals, in Europe, there are also beggars. Transiting from feudalism to industrialization in Europe, there were peasants; there were beggars in London, in Paris in Warsaw or elsewhere. Each time this cycle begins again; but those with no economic power, those who are not adapted yet to modernity, accept the religion and feel left for account. In addition, they are based either on the religions or on the ethics of solidarity which, more and more, finance begging; but it is not an immutable law which regulates life, all is in perpetual motion.

OB: But according to the Islamic precepts begging is something which must exist because it serves a function.

SE: That is false.

OB: Doesn't that serve any function? If the beggars did not exist, to whom does one have to give?

SE: No, that is false. Islam is never known like that. Islam never legalized begging. Islam has a design for a tax called "sada."

OB: The sadaq.

SE: This other form of begging is not in Islam. It is an exploitation that emanated from Islam but not in Islam. Alms, you can give on Friday to the mosque what you want. At the end of the year, you must leave something. You must to give to the Imam. It is the Imam who knows the needy ones and gives them with decency and dignity.

OB: I am in agreement with what you have just said on the gift of the zakat but it is said that in Saudi Arabia, there are no beggars because everyone obeys the Koranic regulation on the zakat very well. One obeys the regulation to the letter and one gives until one finds no beggar in the street.

SE: Yes, yes.

OB: In this light are you in agreement that the presence of beggars on our streets in Africa (and Asia) must lie with the fact that the rich Moslems in our continent do not give enough as had been prescribed in Islam?

SE: No, it is not at all the question either. It is the refusal. Islam does not accept that. Good, let us go further. Haven't we said that many African heads of state today on a journey in Europe asking for money have engaged in another form of begging?

OB: Yes, Nigeria for example.

SE: But it is not Nigeria alone. Not because Nigeria is your country. At some point the people or the heads of states must assume responsibility to solve their own problems themselves. This is what I want to you to comprehend. Poverty exists but I do not know any who dares to say poverty is absolute in Africa.

OB: That is quite true. But it is not that I myself rationalize begging; the Islamic religion for example

158

regards a form of begging as sanctioned. Yes, I believe...
i.e., that the practice to go to search alms in....

SE: It is not a question of to go to search... It is not
worthwhile to go to search, one must wait....

OB: Until one is given.

SE: That is it.

OB: And if they do not give, how...?

SE: No, if they do not give it is another thing. It is
when one leaves his house to go to ask, it is when one
goes against the method to receive alms... the Islamic
religion made the distribution of the things well. Begging
initially even should be, if one is a good Moslem,
avoided because at length, that becomes humiliation. And
then it is not right...

OB: To do what?

SE: It is not right to refuse to give. One must give to
the mosque through the Imam who divides the gifts. One
cannot, on the other hand, forget it in discretion.

OB: So the zakat is always obligatory.

SE: Yes.

OB: One must pay it.

SE: Yes, but another must not go to seek it.

OB: But if it is not paid, how will the beggars live?

SE: It is not a problem. You go to the Imam who
knows his parishioners. You donate. They are circulated.
Otherwise one must find a useful work. But begging in
our streets rises from the spirit or the idea that it is a
moral obligation with a preceding good purpose. It is not
true. You do not do it to feed people but to be enriched in
the other form of existence, in the other better world.

OB: Considering its importance in the life of those who give, don't you believe that it also has a poignant influence on their psychology?

SE: Yes, yes it is an obligation and all the religions have it that either (Catholic) Christian or Moslem, in the cathedrals of Europe, there are beggars.

OB: Very well.

SE: In China too. But it is necessary to pose the question why there are people deprived, people who do not have anything, but do not commit suicide. Why? Why, I ask you the question.

OB: Why what?

SE: Why do they not commit suicide, why? I ask you the question.

OB: Please I do not understand the question well.

SE: Why do the poor, wretched and deprived not commit suicide?

OB: They do not commit suicide because they believe that they can arrive in life with some effort, i.e. they are not resigned to the problem, the situation; they always seek a chance, an opening, out of the problem.

SE: You see. You see now that begging is transitory.

OB: Yes, it is; it is transitory at the individual level.

SE: You see.

OB: What is the goal of the fight which your beggars in your book carried out?

SE: It is for you to read and say about them what you want. Eh?....It is not for me. It is for the readers.

OB: You believe that a disabled person, a beggar, can carry out a revolution of itself?

SE: Why? Is that still a question I must answer for you?

OB: According to Marxist dialectic, the fight against the middle-class must be carried out through weapons. You believe that a beggar, actually, can awake one beautiful day and make war with the authorities, the middle-class?

SE: Listen, it is a metaphor, you see?

OB: What is the end, the goal of this metaphor?

SE: A beggar, the beggars, can make a revolution. The beggars can make a moral revolution. They initiate a process that can lead to a revolution....They all are of the citizenry. I ask you a question: in a democratic country where everyone has right to vote, do the beggars have the right to vote? Yes or no?

OB: Yes, they have it perfectly. That it is quite true.

SE: And then... why do you believe that they cannot make a revolution like the other members of the society? In any case they are more numerous, more in these countries, ready for a revolution.

OB: What do you think of the new tendency where the beggars oblige the men to give them alms?

SE: I do not get it....

OB: What do you think of the new tendency where in the big cities like Dakar, Lagos, Kano... the beggars oblige the authorities to give them alms?

SE: From beginning they know their force, numerical and moral, and the others have a bad conscience of it.

OB: Where in *Xala* is work symbolic of the system?

SE: It is for you to see. ... It is not for me. It is for you to analyze. It is not for me...

SE: If one draws up a chart from reading *Xala*, one will realise two broad themes: the problem of neocolonialism and that of begging. Is it necessary to see these topics like different or complementary?

SE: Can one separate from the same water-bottle warm water and cool water? That is the problem in *Xala*.

OB: The outcome of *Xala* illustrates "the dictatorship of the proletariat", but there is no proletariat in the novel, owing to the fact that the beggars do not work. What do you want to show there, a simple idealization?

SE: It is symbolism.

OB: What is the goal of this symbolism?

SE: That is for you to analyze. Me, I simply write and leave you make of them what you want to.

OB: How do you place yourself compared to the other Senegalese writers like Aminata Sow Fall in *The Beggars' Strike,* Nafissatou Diallo in *De Tilène au Plateau* and Ly Sangare in *Sourd-Muet*?

SE: There, it is you who place me. I do not place myself...

OB: But there is something which binds you, you four in these works.

SE: But *Xala* came before all these other works, see?

OB: From talks with Senegalese friends, I have learned that *De Tilène au Plateau* also strives to depict the place where the poor live, the lowly people.

SE: No, no, when Dakar was not also a big city, there was Lanes, see?

OB: Yes.

SE: Here you see... it is like Gueye Wayne, The *Valley of Salted* Pond, etc.

OB: Yes.

SE: It is simply a process of basic conflict, fine. But as any metropolis develops the shopping malls, they attract all of the poor. In Lagos, there are "poor districts" and also "rich districts"

OB: It is so.

SE: But it is the expansion of the city that does that.

OB: Yes but from the title of the novel, *De Tilène au Plateau*, one already sees a conflict.

SE: Yes.

OB: And this conflict exists from beginning to end of the text.

SE: Yes.

OB: As in *Xala*, there is a conflict between the poor districts and the rich districts in *De Tilène au Plateau* i.e., an opposition of poor suburbs to the rich city. Don't you see a kind of parallelism in this process of conflict?

SE: It is for you. It is for you who studied the three books to make the analysis.

OB: Moussa in his above mentioned novel shows the process of emancipation of a beggar, a beggar who in spite of his infirmity, asks for the word… he wants to be understood by the people.

SE: Yes.

OB: Don't you see the same plot in *Xala*?

SE: That also is for you to analyze; it is you who do the research.

OB: How do you characterize the fight which opposes your beggars against the authorities in the novel?

SE: It is in the book. It is the subject of the book. When they came to the house… to invade the house...

OB: It is clear in *God's Bits of Woods* and *Xala* the outcome is always an attack on the residence of the oppressors. Why this leaning?

SE: It is for you to compare. Since the beginning up to now, people fight and, since they fight, it is necessary that they arrive at victory.

OB: The victory of these beggars in the novel, can you regard it as a real victory itself because, after all, the beggars can never set up a government or...

SE: Yes, yes.

OB: A system of organization.

SE: What did the beggars do to El Hadji in *Xala*? They stripped him, ridiculed him and asked him whether he wanted to become a man....

OB: Yes, they humiliated him, derided him.

SE: It is necessary that he is punished.

OB: Yes.

SE: The beggars will not go away; only they will confront the corrupt people. They will go with the intellectuals of the country; they will go to victory with the workmen. That is completely a metaphor, the Marxist metaphor if one can say.

OB: In other words, they mobilize the others who are not corrupt, who go to make war....

SE: Yes.

OB: Against those who are corrupt?

SE: It is precisely that.

OB: Throughout the novel you speak of beggars only in the singular. What is the significance to use only one beggar? Each time you make allusions to the beggar, "the beggar", "the beggar..." until the end of the novel why the reference to only one?

SE: Because, if I had said "the beggars" that would not be well recorded in your head but, in the singular, when I say "the beggar", "the beggar", "the beggar", that remains in your head. Did you notice that they are very numerous? There is always a head.

OB: Oh… to carry out a revolution?

SE: There you are.

OB: When you speak about begging in *Xala*, is it begging in itself that you denounce or is it only one symbol of laziness to be denounced in our society of today?

SE: It is not the same thing. It is the sins of El Hadji, Abdou Kader Bèye. It has its wages. He became impotent. He could not lay with his wife. It is the symbol of the impotence of the black middle-class. And men as El Hadji are nothing but the rest of them.

OB: By extension, don't you believe that this symbol, this impotence known under the name of xala, also affects the beggars themselves insofar as they prove to be impotent, ineffective in the revolutionary fight?

SE: Undoubtedly not.

OB: Don't you see that they prove to be impotent from the awkward way by which they had carry out the fight? Don't you believe that they are impotent because they did not carry out the rather proletarian fight in a revolutionary way as it is necessary?

SE: No, they are not proletarians.

OB: Yes, but...

SE: They are not workmen.

OB: It is so but...

SE: Did you see *The Revolt of the Peasants*?

OB: Yes.

SE: You already saw *The Revolt of the Peasants*?

OB: Yes.

SE: They do not act like workmen either.

165

OB: Do you believe in destiny?

SE: Very well.

OB: Do you believe that all that a man is in this life - low or high - is predestined?

SE: Fate.

OB: Yes, fate.

SE: Fate, oh no.

OB: According to you, where is the connection between man and destiny?

SE: It is man who makes his destiny. There is no connection.

OB: Please what anecdotic interpretation can you give to *Xala*? Because me, I read *Xala* like an anecdote, and also, like facts.

SE: Me, I write and I do not put myself to questions. I do not have the disease of proof. I put questions to my society. What is the simplest form to touch the widest of public possible? That is the problem.

OB: In other words, an interpretation centred on the reader.

SE: Yes, but in essence it is a matter of comprehension; there is in the same book several visions. Do you understand me?

OB: Yes...

SE: You, you have pointed out two of them but there are others ....I have seen readers who point out three or even four. Perhaps because me, I am not conscious of all that I put in a book.

OB: Throughout the novel, the only weapon of the beggar is "his song". And that bites, in a painful way, the authorities represented by El Hadji Abdou Kader Bèye. What does this song mean?

SE: It is difficult to distinguish the colour of water from the pond but falling drop by drop on the stone it can perforate a piece of iron.... It is so. If not, why the beggar, the beggar, the beggar? Must he sing differently from the raison d'être his destiny had forced upon him?

OB: The beggar in the novel prides himself to control the fate of El Hadji and it is fate which makes one weak and the other strong. Don't you believe that the way of being avenged in secrecy with the help of sorcery is anti-revolutionist?

SE: What?

OB: Do you not believe that to be avenged by manipulating fate is anti-revolutionist?

SE: No, that is not the most important passage in the book. You know in our society, people are passive and do not like to work.... Do you agree or not?

OB: They are passive.

SE: Yes, and it is this passivity which causes the problem.

OB: Don't you believe that the way in which the beggar was avenged is anti-revolutionist?

SE: No, there is not a single, fixed manner to carry out a revolution.

OB: But according to Marx, there is a...

SE: Listen, the society evolves. Marx wrote at the time a scientific book about London or Germany but more about London....Good. China made its revolution in its own way. Vietnam in fact had her revolution in its own way. Cuba made its revolution the same way... and Mozambique, Angola, Zimbabwe... one should not take the revolution as solidified, it is necessary to be able to adapt from Marxism, which is a science, one of its aspects which does not belong any more to anybody.

OB: Thus one can domesticate Marxism in one's own way.

SE: Yes, yes, in one's own way, on the basis of one's own realities.

OB: So far so good. On page 163 of the novel you said and I quote: "Did the beggar always direct a similar operation?" Can you tell me in which work of arts, personal, critical or sociological where beggars played the part of invaders?

SE: They are not invaders. I do not like the word because then you seem to protect the private property —when you say that they invade the private property.

OB: Yes....

SE: But any private property of a certain dimension implies struggle and exploitation of the sweat of others, right?

OB: Of course, one can describe their role like that of militants.

SE: Very well, militant role, that goes.

OB: On page 170 of the novel, we see a disabled person ordering Adja Awa Astou (wife of El Hadji) to spit in the eyes of her husband, El hadji Abdou Kader Bèye. Why do you use a disabled person, and still a woman, in this manner? Is this to further the work of female liberation?

SE: Yes, because Africa cannot develop or make the revolution, without the participation of the women. They are more than half of the population. Yes, they are more than half.

OB: According to what you have just said, can we draw the conclusion that it is to this end, perhaps, that you made the educated girl of El Hadji say to the police who came to arrest the beggars in his residence that they are "the guests of dad"?

SE: Yes.

OB: Thus they can also take part (by doing this) in the revolution of society. Is it?

SE: Yes, it is.

OB: They take part with the beggars in the new crusade to purge the society of dishonest individuals.

SE: Yes, they are... how do you say that in the university?

OB: Progressive.

SE: Yes.

OB: Thus the new vision of the world of the beggars is just as that of the educated feminists.

SE: And yet the beggars did not go to school.

OB: Yet their situation revolts them.

SE: Yes.

OB: This is to say that it is their state of begging, their condition, which obliges them in spite of diversities of their forms, their state. It is the condition which joins them together in a common front.

SE: Yes, there.

OB: What do you mean by making the beggar say (on page 169) that in the country where he lived, the prisoner is happier than the workman and the peasant?

SE: Yes, yes.

OB: What do you want to say by that?

SE: Yes, look at our current society, Nigeria, Senegal, Mali, etc. The prisoner is fed and kept safe.

OB: Yes.

SE: When he is sick, he is taken care of. The peasant does not have that; the workman does not have that. The workman must work to the pain of death.

OB: Do you mean that in the current difficult economic situation which we suffer it is better to be a prisoner than a workman: better to go begging because then one will enjoy things which one would not have the privilege even if one worked?

SE: That is not for me to say. The beggars know, not me. I know that in our present African countries the prisoners live better than the beggars do.

OB: In other words,

SE: They drink very freely. They eat and when they are sick one looks after them and they do not pay a tax. They do not have to be even worried –the prisoners.

OB: In other words, if I understand you well, in the absence of thrush, one eats the blackbird.

SE: Yes.

OB: Or if one does not manage to have work for one becomes prisoner....

SE: No, it is not that one must be a prisoner. For Marx, it is a kind of parallel which he made and which is true. You know... in the film "Xala", this passage was censored in Senegal and thus it was removed, cut out.

OB: Oh... because of this passage which I have just quoted?

SE: Yes, yes.

OB: It was cut out of reel?

SE: Yes, it was cut out.

OB: The Senegalese penal code prohibits begging. Is it begging in itself which is proscribed or the way in which people beg?

SE: Well, if it was formerly prohibited, it cannot be prohibited begging in the current situation any more.

OB: What kind of society would you like to see existing in Africa?

SE: Scientific Socialist.

OB: With the Marxists...?

SE: But adapted to our realities. It would be neither Chinese socialism nor Russian.

OB: That is to say, Socialism conceived according to African realities.

SE: Yes, yes.

OB: Why the translation of text to screen, the translation of the novel...

SE: To the image?

OB: Yes.

SE: Me, I prefer the books, but the majority do not read and the books are expensive, while everyone goes to the cinema.

OB: Thus it is from an economic standpoint that you made this adaptation.

SE: Yes... yes, because of those who did not read the book. It is in my book, *The Mandate*. It is not in *Xala*.

OB: Begging is a problem; what can you propose for its solution?

SE: I do not know. It is necessary to change the society. Everyone can produce. Yes, everyone. The society can use all the valid hands, and then perhaps we would not have any more beggars. The one who begs is not proud. No woman, no man likes to beg yes, in any country of the world.

OB: Doesn't begging in *The Mandate* go in the same direction as that described in *Xala*?

SE: No, it is different.

OB: What is the difference?

SE: You should find out.

OB: I have searched but it can be seen that in *The Mandate* the women of Ibrahima Dieng beg to feed themselves because their husband is poor; in *Xala* also, people are obliged to beg to contain the hunger. So I'm afraid it is the same begging.

SE: Yes, it is the same objective yet the situation grows increasingly bad. In Africa, if attention is not paid, we will have more of beggars than peasants and workmen.

OB: In other words, all these two works, *The Mandate* and *Xala*, seem to be signals, warnings.

SE: For our countries.

OB: So that they can take some action.

SE: Yes. What actions should be taken? It is clear that when we arrest, or raid the beggars and disperse them, they return. Yes, they return because of the famine where you can only hope to eat; I did not say that you find what to eat, but you hope to eat.

OB: Because the city with its problems, or its difficulties, is better than the village?

SE: Yes.

OB: But the African governments of today encourage the policy of return to grassroots. Do you not believe that such a policy is more promising than false hopes to find fortune in the cities?

SE: It is quite beautiful to promise, to say to people "go to countryside" but when they return to the countryside, the ground does not yield any more, people die, the children die, the animals die... the disease.... What will one make of these?

OB: ... ...

SE: Eh? ... I ask you the question. What will one make of these? You will remain on the spot?

OB: No, I am obliged to go into the cities.

SE: There you are.

OB: Sir, *The Radiance of the King* by Camara Laye...

SE: Yes.

OB: It spoke about a beggar, but it did not capture the image of this beggar well.

SE: Yes?

OB: The manner in which he introduced this beggar; it is as if the beggar really has a power.

SE: Yes, it is in the subconscious of people.

OB: The marabout in *The Radiance of the King*...

SE: Yes, *The Radiance of the King* is far back.

OB: It goes back to 1954.

SE: It was few years before independence then. Eh? The villages had a beggar who is a well-read type....he can recite the Koran.

OB: Yes, he works in the court of the king.

SE: Like what?

OB: Like a guard.

SE: Here, very true. That is not the beggar who goes to beg.

OB: It is an advanced beggar.

SE: Yes.

OB: Which is to say that all works which speak about the beggar after 1954 only try to recapture this image of a great beggar?

SE: No, that was the image of the beggar presented in a purely African feudal society.

OB: Oh, the image of beggar presented in...

SE: *The Radiance of the King* yes. It is in the feudal period.

OB: Yes, and the form of begging described in *Xala* is in the modern capitalist system.

SE: Yes, they are in the city and the struggle is harder.

OB: Can one say that the beggar introduced in *The Radiance of the King* is cynical and philosophical?

SE: Yes, blindness is not begging.

OB: Blindness, sir?

SE: Yes.

OB: Is the beggar there blind?

SE: Yes.

OB: But he played a very dominating part. He could order the white man Clarence around– just as your beggar did to El Hadji Abdou Kader Bèye.

SE: You are right.

END

Notes and Bibliography

Chapter 1
Re-visioning African Writing

NOTES

1As in the mission statement of the International Research Council on African Literature and Culture, IRCALC, <http://www.africaresearch.org>

2The triad of Chinweizu, Onwuchekwa Jemie and Ihechukwu Madubuike had published in Transition series of treatises that instigated a major revision of the literary canons when they culminated in a stunning polemical but visionary compendium published 1980 as Toward the Decolonisation of African Literature.

3Taken from Camara Laye's biographical novel: A Dream of Africa, an idea consistent with Laye's central African vision which his critics had often and unfairly taken to mean a servitude to French colonial imperialism.

4Many scholars will agree, of course, that the tragedy or series of unremitting disaster in Oil Man of Obange told by John Munonye belongs more in classical Greek tradition than African or Igbo traditions where men are seen to dialogue with the gods in order to change or ameliorate their destinies for the better.

5Soyinka's dramas around Brother Jero, the cavalier character that triumphs rather than meets his doom in The Jero Plays and Sanda, a 'resurrection' of Jero in the eighties Beatification of Area Boy, are not so much satires of religious charlatanism or military autocracy as they are a triumph of the bohemian drama of social redemption via nonconformist but truly visionary realism.

6A further example of Soyinka's African vision comes with the Western educated son of the Elesin Oba in Death and the King's Horseman, who returns from England to perform traditional rites in honour of his father the Elesin Oba, but is constrained to carry out the sacred duty of accompanying his dead king to the great beyond when his father fails in this duty. It installs, in the opinion of this treatise, a quality lacking in the self-seeking modernism of post colonial African societies being the deeper sense of allegiance to a spiritual bond, an instinct always in readiness to let go of lower self interest for the survival of the whole and greater continuum.

7This is Achebe's own opinion of Camara's African world, in the autobiographical work translated The African Child in English, which is opposed to the more balanced Africa of Okonkwo's tragic destiny in Things Fall Apart.

8For Nigerian writing, we tend to consider Chukwuemeka Ike's The Potter's Wheel and Sunset at Dawn, Ifeoma Okoye's Behind the Clouds, Mariama Ba's So Long a Letter, Isidore Okpewho's The Last Duty and Akachi Ezeigbo's Children of the Eagle, among many other later works of this period, as revisions of the trend in modern pessimist and cynic realist writing to that of emerging hopeful transcendence that has yet to be fully and creatively explored by present generation of Nigerian writers.

9Predictably Immanuel Velikovsky's theory in Worlds in Collision (1956) that the events recorded in Exodus were not God's vengeance on Egypt for persecuting His 'chosen' people, but parts of series of a worldwide upheaval involving collisions between the planets which were felt and recorded in still extant annals of human history, convulsed, till the present, the Christian world of Europe and America to unimaginable proportions of blackmail and vilification of the lifelong research of that great physicist.

10Achebe's famous proverb in Arrow of God popularised by the Nigerian literary critic Ernest Emenyonu in a publication on new critical perspectives on African literature entitled Goatskin Bags and Wisdom.

WORKS CITED

Achebe, Chinua. "Chi in Igbo Cosmogony." Morning Yet on Creation day. Ibadan: London: Heinemann, 1975.

– – –. "Tanganyinka:–Jottings of a Tourist." Morning Yet on Creation day. London: Heinemann, 1975.

– – –. No Longer at Ease. Ibadan: Heinemann. 1960.

Bressler, Charles. Introduction to Literary Criticism. New Jersey: Paramount, 1994.

Clement, H. A. The Story of the Ancient World. London: Africa Universities Press, 1936.

Conwell, Russell. "Acres of Diamonds." Connecticut: Keats Publishing Inc., 1972.

Coullie, Judith Lütge (ed). The Closest of Strangers: South African Women's Writing. Johannesburg: Witts University Press, 2001.

Eko, Ebele. Elechi Amadi: The Man and his Work. Lagos: Kraft Books, 1991.

Griffith, Tom. "Analysis." The Republic. Plato, Hertfordshire: Wordsworth Classics, 1977.

Nnolim, Charles. "Trends in the Nigerian Novel." Literature and National Consciousness. Ed. Ernest Emenyonu. Ibadan: Heinemann, 1989.

Nwamuo, Chris. Lamentations: Collected Poems. Owerri: AP Publications, 1992.

Osofisan, Femi. Another Raft. Lagos: Malthouse Press, 1988.

Palmer, Eustace. Studies on the African Novel. Ibadan: African Universities Press, 1986.

Soyinka, Wole. Myth, Literature and the African World. London: Cambridge University Press, 1976.

Velikovsky, Immanuel. Preface. Worlds in Collision. New York: Pocket Books, 1950.

Vincent, Theo. "Introduction." Black and African Writing. Ed. Theo Vincent. Lagos: CBAAC, 1981.

Weiss, Bettina. "Shades of Utter(ing) Silences in The Purple Violet of Oshaantu, Maru, and Under the Tongue." Journal of African Literature and Culture 4. 2007.13-32.

Chapter 2
The Folktale in Achebe's Fictions

NOTES

1Ruth Finnegan, Oral Literature in Africa (Nairobi: CUP) 1976, Emmanuel Obiechina, Cultural, Tradition and in the African Novel (Cambridge: OUP) 1975, Bernth Lindfors, Folklore in Nigerian Literature (NY: Africana) 1973, Isidore Okpewho, The Epic in Africa: Towards a Poetic of the Oral Performance (NY: Columbia Univ Press) 1979.

2Zubus borrows Alianne Tine's term 'ethno-text' to refer to the oral forms transposed to the written text. Chantal Zubus, "The Logos Eaters: The Igbo Ethno_Text," Chinua Achebe: A Celebration (ed) Kirsten Holst Petersen & Anna Rutherford (Oxford: Heinemann) 1991, p 20 ; Chinweizu et al object to the employment of Eurocentric categories like epic, romance and so on in the classification of the fictional narratives of the non-western world. The major part of Chinweizu's argument is to establish the difference between orature and scripture as that of the medium. pp 10-86. The African Novel and its Critics, p.28;

Henry Louis Gates Jr regards the Talking Book as the ur trope of Anglo American tradition and shows that the "curious tension between the black vernacular and the literate white text, between the spoken and the written word, between the oral and the printed form of literary discourse has been thematized in black letters." But like the Afro-American or West Indian the black persons "could become speaking subjects only by inscribing their voices in the written word." Henry Louis Gates Jr, "The Blackness of Blackness: A critique of the Sign and the Signifying Monkey," Critical Inquiry, Vol 9, No4 p131; The "Manichean allegory that JanMohammed sees as scaffolding colonialist literature fetishizes the other, not only to "maintain a sense of moral difference" but also to pass off socio-historical difference as biological"; Abdul R JanMohammed, "The Economy of Manichean

Allegory: The Function of Racial Difference in Colonial Literature", Critical Inquiry, Vol 12, No 1, 1985, p.21.

R Sundara Rajan, "Phenomenology and Language: The Last Frontier", Studies in Humanities and Social Sciences, Vol II, No 2, 1996, p.49.

5ibid, p.48.

6ibid, p.49.

7Albert Gerard, "Preservation of Tradition in African Creative Writing", RAL, Vol 1, No 1, Spring 1970, p 36; Chinweizu et al, contending that written literature had a long tradition Africa, testify to the existence of written literature in parts of Africa, like Ethiopia and Sudan, dating earlier than many parts of Europe. Chinweizu maintains that writing traveled from these regions of the Nile Valley to the Mediterranean cultures of Crete, Greece etc, p.26.

8Chinua Achebe, Things Fall Apart: The African Trilogy (London: Heinemann Picador), 1998.

9Chinua Achebe, Arrow of God (London: Heinemann Picador), 1998.

10 Levi-Strauss, Claude. Myth and Meaning. London: Routledge, 2001. 6

11 Obiechina argues that Achebe himself provides signposts for reading the novel, rendering background information superfluous. Emmanuel Obiechina, "Following the Author in Things Fall Apart", Approaches to Teaching Achebe's Things Fall Apart (ed) B Lindfors (NY: MLA) 1991, p.31. Obiechina observes that even literate West Africans continue to share the values, attitudes and structures of feeling implicit within their culture. He points out that a purely oral culture embodies its values and attitudes in proverbs and sayings, beliefs in its myths and religion, consciousness of its historical life, collective outlook and ethics in its legends and folktales, Culture, Tradition and Society in the West African Novel, p.27.

12 Visnusarma, Panchatantra, tr and introduced by Chandra Rajan (N Delhi: Penguin) 1993.

14 Compare it with the old adage in Panchatantra:

With mere booklearning men remain fools
the man who act using his knowledge, he is wise
(II.109.1,2)

15Obiechina observes that even literate West Africans continue to share the values, attitudes and structures of feeling implicit within their culture. He points out that a purely oral culture embodies its values and attitudes in proverbs and sayings, beliefs in its myths and religion, consciousness of its historical life, collective outlook and ethics in its legends and folktales, p.27; Similarly Chinweizu et al, objecting to the dismissal of the spiritual/ supernatural in the African novel as "primitive" in eurocentric criticism, testify to the belief in the supernatural as prevalent among the bourgeois. p 20; Paulin Houndantji critiques the word ethnophilosophy and warns that the dangers of imposing "as a norm, in Africa what was actually a deviation in relation to the theoretical practices predominating in Europe itself in the native cultures of the promoters of this supposed norm". (112) Paulin Houndantji has called attention to the ambiguity in the use of terms like "ethnoscience" or "ethnophilosophy". The prefix could be used either to connote pre existing knowledge, knowledge in civilizations based on orality and the application of the method of a given science to some aspect of a "primitive" culture. (113) He objects to the appropriation of the cultures of orality by the ethnologist showing them to be incapable of being represented except in the language of the West. (117) Paulin Houndantji, "From the Ethnosciences to Ethnophilosophy: Kwame Nkrumah's Thesis Project," RAL,Vol 28, No 4, Winter 1997, pp 112-20.

16Edith Tarcor (comp) The Portable Saul Bellow (NY: The Viking Press) p.288.

17Chinua Achebe, "Chi in Igbo Cosmology," Morning Yet on Creation Day London: Heinemann, 1975.

18Bernth Lindfors, "Folktale as Paradigm in Arrow of God", Critical Perspectives on Chinua Achebe. Ed C.L. Innes and Bernth Lindfors. London: Heinemann, 1979.

19 Mary Ellen B Lewis, "Beyond Content in the Analysis of Folklore in Literature: Chinua Achebe's Arrow of God." Research in African Literatures. Vol 7. No 1. pp.44-52.

20 Barbara Harlow, "The Tortoise and the Birds: Strategies of Resistance in Things Fall Apart." Approaches to Teaching Things Fall Apart, op.cit., p.75.

21 Cathy Ramadan & Donald Weinstock, "Symbolic Structure in Things Fall Apart." Critical Perspectives on Chinua Achebe (ed.) C L Innes & Bernth Lindfors (London: Heinemann) 1979, pp.126-34.

22 Onmeynou B Traore, "Matrical Approach to Things Fall Apart." Ed. Bernth Lindfors. NY: MLA, 1991.

23 Emmanuel Obiechina, "Narrative Proverbs in the African Novel." RAL, Winter 1993, Vol.24, No. 4.

24 R Sundara Rajan borrows Horton's categories of personalistic and naturalistic to describe points of view that personalize events and those that explain them in abstract and objective terms respectively. Horton had, in fact, seen the African as an example of the personalistic.

25 The bard narrates the tale of the love of Ares and Aphrodite. Homer, The Odyssey (trans) E V Rieu (Harmondsworth: Penguin) 1976, p.129.

26 Jan Mukarovsky, The Word and Verbal Art trans and ed by John Burnank and Peter Steiner (New Haven: Yale Univ Press) 1977, pp.180-204.

27 See Rems Nna Umeasiegbu, The Way we Lived (London: Heinemann) 1977. Ikemefuna is another born storyteller who retells known tales with a new freshness and the local flavour of a different clan.(40)

28 Though Obiechina dwells on the call-and-response poetics in the tales used by Achebe, he feels that the written nature of the novel reduces, if not eliminates, their paralinguistic features. Obiechina, op. cit., p.127.

29 ibid, 125.

30Sundara Rajan quotes Habermas: "What we find most astonishing is the peculiar leveling of the different domains of reality: nature and culture are projected on the same plane. From this reciprocal assimilation of nature to culture and conversely of culture to nature, these results, on one hand, a nature that utilized anthropocentric features and is in this sense humanized and a culture that is to a certain extent naturalized." Sundara Rajan, op.cit., p 47; Abiola Irele speaks of the fusion of Fagunwa's world "into a comprehensive theatre of the human drama of the natural and supernatural realms," which he locates in the Yoruba conception of the universe that allows the coexistence of the natural with the supernatural." Abiola Irele, "Tradition and the Yoruba Writer: D O Fagunwa, Amos Tutuola and Wole Soyinka," Critical Perspectives on Wole Soyinka (ed) James Gibbs (London: Three Continents Press) 1980, p.50; Chinweizu, Jamie and Madubuike speak of the secular rational outlook of the European novel as antithetical to the "supernatural" perspective of African narratives and cosmology.

31Cf. Obiechina to see the importance of the story in African discursive and socio-philosophical writings, Obiechina, op.cit., p 124. Chinua Achebe, "Chi in Igbo Cosmology, op.cit., pp.93-103.

32 Finnegan, op.cit, pp.44-79.

33 Achebe, "Chi in Igbo Cosmology," op.cit, 96-97.

34John Mbiti, African Religions and Philosophy (London: Heinemann) 1970, p.21.

35According to Mbiti, (1970) a distinction is made in African time between the past recalled by the oldest member of the village and the collective memory of the past that cannot be ascribed to any particular individual.

36The debate between Charles A. Nnolim and Bu-Buakei Jabbi on the question of plagiarism and originality with reference to Achebe's use of the Nnolim text in Arrow of God refers to this openness of the oral text. Bu Buakei Jabbi, "Myth and Ritual in Arrow of God." African Literature Today No 11(London: Heinemann) 1980, pp.130-47.

37Chinua Achebe, "No Longer at Ease," The African Trilogy, op.cit.

38Chinua Achebe, Anthills of the Savannah, ibid.

Chapter 3
Oral Dynamics of Things Fall Apart

WORKS CITED

Achebe, Chinua. Things Fall Apart. London: Heinemann, 1958.

Ajadi, Gabriel. "African Oral Literature: Definition, Theory and Taxonomy." The English Language and Literature in English: An Introductory Handbook. Ed. Efurosibina Adegbija. Ilorin: Department of Modern European Languages, 1999. 235-248.

Awonoor, Kofi . The Breast of the Earth. New York: Nok Publishers Int., 1975.

Bamidele, 'Dele. "Awonoor's Myth of 'Archetypal Scapegoating' in This Earth, My Brother: A Reflection." Anyigba Journal of Arts & Humanities. 1.2. 2001. 10- 17.

Bodunde, Charles. Oral Traditions and Aesthetic Transfer: Creativity and Social Vision in Contemporary Black Poetry. Bayreuth: BASS, 2001.

Chinweizu, Onwuchekwa Jemie and Ihechukwu Madubuike. Towards the Decolonization of African Literature. Vol. 1. Enugu: Fourth Dimension, 1980.

Egejuru, Phanuel. "Oratory Okwu Oka: A Neglected Technique in Achebe's Literary Artistry." Eagle on Iroko. Ed. Edith Ihekweazu. Ibadan: Heinemann, 1996. 394- 410.

Lindfors, Bernth. Folktale in Nigerian Literature. U.S.A: Africana Publishing Company, 1973.

Na'Allah, Abdulrasheed. "Oral Literary Tradition in Africa." New Introduction to Literature. Ed. Olu Obafemi. Ibadan: Y-Books, 1994. 101- 118.

Ogunjimi, Bayo. "Journey Artifice and Orature: Idioms in Three Revolutionary African Novels". Alore: Ilorin Journal of the Humanities. 6-8. 1990, 1992. 50- 62.

Ohaeto, Ezenwa. "Structural Synthesis: Oral Traditions in the Novels of Chukwuemeka Ike." Chukwuemeka Ike: A Critical Reader. Ed. Kanchana Ugbabe. Lagos: Malthouse, 2001.

Ojaide, Tanure. "Poetry, Performance and Art: Udje Dance Songs of Nigeria's Urhobo People." Research in African Literatures. 32.2. 2001: 44- 75.

Qusseynou, Traore. "The Narrative Grammar of Things Fall Apart: Gender and Structural Functions of The Mosquito Myth." Eagle on Iroko. Ibadan: Heinemann, 1996. 323- 345.

Sugnet, Charlie. "Things Fall Apart: Problems In Constructing An Alternative Ethnography." Eagle on Iroko. Ibadan: Heinemann, 1996.85- 94.

Umeasiegbu, Rems. "Folktales in the Novels of Chinua Achebe." Faculty Seminar Series Paper, Kogi State University, Anyigba, 2002.

Chapter 4
Orality in the Works of Ousmane Sembène

WORKS CITED

Aas-Rouxparis, Nicole. "Conversation with Ousmane Sembène." The French Review, Vol. 75, No. 3 (May 1997), 571-577.

Bakupa-Kanyinda, Balufu. "Challenging Stereotypes." UN Chronicle, March-May, 2003. www.findarticles.com

Cham, Mbye. African Experiences of Cinema. London: British Film Institute, 1996.

Diop, Abdoulaye Bara. La Socièté wolof: tradition et changement, les systèmes d'inégalité et de domination. Paris: Karthatla, 1981.

Gadjigo, Samba. "Ousmane Sembène: The Life of a Revolutionary Artist." Mount Holyoke College. <www.newsreel.org/articles/OusmaneSembène.htm> 11/4/2005.

Laye, Camara. Le Maître de la parole: Kouma lafôlô kouma. Paris: Plon, 1978.

Murphy, David. Sembène: Imagining Alternatives in Film and Fiction. Oxford: James Currey Ltd., 2001.

Niang, Sada. "La Notion de caste chez les Wolofs: mythe ou histoire?" African Continuities/L'Héritage Africaine. Eds. Simeon W. Chilungu and Sada Niang. Toronto: Terebi, 1989.

Nzbatsinda, Anthère. "Le Griot dans le récit d'ousmane Sembène: entre la rupture et la continuité d'une représentation de la parole africaine." The French Review, 70, 6. May, 1997. 865-872.

Pfaff, Françoise. "The Uniqueness of Ousmane Sembène's Cinema." Ousmane Sembène: Dialogues with Critics and Writers. Eds. Gadjigo, Faulkingham, Cassirer. Amherst: University of Massachusetts Press, 1993. 14-21.

Rapfogel, Jared. "Ousmane Sembène: Senegal's Master of Cinema." <www.far-and-near.com/cin_lit/Sembène.htm> 10/18/2005.

Sembène, Ousmane. Xala. Paris: Présence Africaine, 1974. English translation: Chicago: Heinemann Books, 1976.

– – –. Voltaique. Paris: Présence Africaine, 1962

– – –. L'Harmattan: référendum. Paris: Présence Africaine, 1975.

Ukadike, Nwachukwu Frank. Black African Cinema. Los Angeles: University of California Press, 1994.

Films:
"Borom Sarret." (In French with English subtitles.) Dir. Ousmane Sembène, 1963

"Xala." (In French and Wolof with English subtitles.) Dir. Ousmane Sembène, 1974

"Ceddo." (In Wolof with English subtitles.) Dir. Ousmane Sembène, 1976

"Faat Kiné." (In French and Wolof with English subtitles.) Dir. Ousmane Sembène, 2001

Chapter 5
Oral Multidimensional Collage in Recent Fiction

NOTES

1Friedrich Nietzsche's Thus Spoke Zarathustra does not only parallel Bozo's journey to the woods like the prophet Zarathustra, it is equally Bozo's reference point in Bandele-Thomas' novel when he declares his atheistic stance before his religious studies teacher, Mrs. Myra Buck and his classmates. He insists that Christ is not the one who inaugurated the Eucharist feast, but a prophet named Mithras Zarathustra, Pp 43, 44,45.

2Daniel Defoe Robinson Crusoe. London: Penguin Classic, 2001.Pp17-19

3DuPlesssis Rachel B. Writing Beyond the Ending: Narrative Strategies of Twentieth Century Women Writers. Bloominton: Indiana Up, 1985

4See Emezue, GMT. "Complementary Realism: Achebe, Ce." New Black and African Writing. Eds. Charles Smith and GMT Emezue. AI: Handel Books, 2009. Pp.237-260

WORKS CITED

Agho, Jude. "Scatology, Form and Meaning in the Fiction of Biyi Bandele-Thomas". Four Decades in the study of Language and Linguistics in Nigeria" A Festchrift for Kay Williamson. Ed. Ozo-Mekuri Ndimele. Aba: NILAN, 2003. 437-447.

Bandele-Thomas, Biyi. The Man who came in from the Back of Beyond. Ibadan: Spectrum, 1991.

Ce, Chin. The Visitor. Enugu: Handel Books, 2004.

Chabel, Patrick and Jean-Pascal Daloz. Africa Works: Disorders as Political instrument.   Oxford: James Carrey, 1999.

Christie, John. Latino Fiction and the Modernist Imagination: Literature of the Borderlands. New York: Garland, 1998

Emery, Mary Lou. Jean Rhys at "World's End": Novels of Colonial and sexual Exile. Austin: University of Texas Press, 1990.

Ezeliora, Osita. "Elegy for the Mystery Cocks: Modern African Literature and the Making of its Classsics." The Postcolonial Lamp: Essays in honour of Dan Izevbaye. Ed. Aderemi Raji-Oyelade and Oyeniyi Okunoye. Ibadan: Bookkraft, 2008. 97-135.

Gasiorek, Andrzej. The Post-War British Fiction: Realism and After. London: Edward Arnold, 1995.

Gaylard, Rob. "Stories and Storytelling in Phaswane Mpe's Welcome to Our Hillbrows" <http://www.uwc.ac.za/arts/auetsa/ gaylard.htm> (12/2/ 2007).

Gray, Stephen. "Third World Meets First World: The Theme of Jim Comes to Joburg in South African English Fiction." Kunapipi 7. 1. 1985. 61-80.

Grants, Amanda. "Memory, Transition and Dialogue: The Cyclic Order of Chin Ce's Oeuvres." Journal of African Literature and Culture. 3. 2006. 11-29.

Haraway, Donna. "A Manisfesto for Cyborgs: Science, Technology, and Socialist Feminism in the 1980s." Socialist Review. 15.2.1985. 65-106.

Harris, Wilson. Selected Essays of Wilson Harris. Ed. Andrew Bundy. London: Routledge,1999.

Kearney, Richard. On Stories: Thinking in Action. London: Routledge, 2002.

Lyotard, Jean-Fancois. The Postmodern Conditions: A Report on Knowledge. Trans. G. Bennington and B. Massumi. Minneapolis: U of Minnesota Press, 1984.

Marques, Irene. "The Works of Chin Ce: A Critical Overview." Critical Supplement: The Works of Chin Ce. Ed. Irene Marques. IRCALC, 2007. 11-36.

Mccabe, Douglas. "'Higher Realities': New Age Spirituality in Ben Okri's The Famished Road." Research in African Literatures. 36. 4. 2005. 1-21.

Mpe, Phaswane. Welcome to Our Hillbrow. Pietermartzburg: University of Natal Press, 2001.

Nkosi, Lewis. Tasks and Masks: Themes and Styles of African Literature. London: Longman, 1981.

Okuyade, Ogaga. The Modernist Temper in the Novels of Dambudzo Marechera and Biyi Bandele-Thomas. M.A. Dissertation, University of Ibadan, 2002.

– – –. "Beyond Anthropological and Historical Rhetoric: Understanding Achebe." Journal of American, British and Canadian Studies. 8. 2007. 228-241.

– – –. "The Rhetoric of Despair in Chin Ce's Children of Koloko."Journal of African Literature and Culture. 4. 2007. 169-186.

– – –."Locating the Voice: The modernist (Postcolonial) Narrative Maze of Chin Ce's The Visitor." Critical Supplement: The Works of Chin Ce. Ed. Irene Marques, IRCALC, 2007: 135-157.

– – –."The Teller in the Tale: Reading Modernist Narrative Strategies in the Novels of Biyi Bandele-Thomas". Volume 5 of the Nigerian Festschrifts Series devoted to Professor Muzulu Jubril. Ed. Ozo-Mekuri Ndimele. Port Harcourt: Linguistic Association of Nigeria , 2007: 519-528.

Qader, Nasrin. "Fictional Testimonies or Testimonial Fictions: Moussa Onld Ebnou's Barzakh". Research in African Literatures. 33, 3. 2002. 14-31.

Saldivar, Ramon. "The Dialectics of Subjectivity: Gender and Difference in Isabella Rios, Sandra Cisneros, and Cherrie Moraga." Chicano Narrative: The Dialectics of Difference. Ed. Ramon Saldivar. Madison: University of Wisconsin Press, 1990: 171-199.

Soyinka, Wole. Myth, Literature and the African World. New York: Canto, 1990.

Vasconelos, Jose. The Cosmic Race: A Bilingual Edition. Trans. Didier T. Jean. Baltimore: Johns Hopkins University Press, 1997.

Watt, Ian. The Rise of the Novel: Studies in Defoe, Richardson and Fielding. Berkeley: U of California Press, 1960.

Wright, Derek. "Pre-and Post-Modernity in Recent West African Fiction" Commonwealth Essay and Studies. 21.2 (1999) 5-17.

Chapter 6
The Mythic Context of Le Jujubier du patriarche

NOTES

1Cf. Christopher Hoagarth in reference to Bhaba, Butler, and Gilroy. "Nomadic Francophonie, Francophone Nomads: The Case of the Senegalese Novel." Contemporary French and Francophone Studies 10.1(2006): 55.

2Published in 1993, Le Jujubier du patriarche is Aminata Sow Fall's fifth novel. The Senegalese author has written seven novels, one of which was awarded the Prix international pour les lettres africaines and two of which have been preselected by the Goncourt jury in Paris.

3Alongside narrative forms and strategies inspired by traditional literature, Aminata Sow Fall's work incorporates oral discourse, thus pointing to the presence of an African symbolic universe in the novel, a genre borrowed from the West. Despite Eileen Julien's contention that any reference to orality in the criticism of African literature smacks of essentialism, Aminata Sow Fall's writing demonstrates continuity with oral literature written in Western languages. In fact many critics agree that the literary text in Africa refers to various texts – oral and traditional as well as written and Western – and is constructed by that reference to other texts. See Julien, African Novels and the Question of Orality (Bloomington : Indiana UP, 1992).

4 According to Jean Dérive, style was one of the primary aspects of works through which the reclamation of alterity was expressed. See Jean Dérive, "Style et fiction d'oralité dans la

narration de quelques romans francophones," Actes du colloque international, Littératures Francophones: Langues et styles (Paris: L'harmattan, 2001) 191. Jean Halen asserts that this style of differencing produces the audibility of the enunciation. See "Les Stratégies francophones du style: l'exemple de quelques sauvages du nord," ibid. 214.

5See Jacques Chevrier, "Présence du mythe dans la littérature africaine contemporaine," Convergences et divergences dans les littératures francophones: Actes du colloque 8-9 février 1991 (Paris: l'Harmattan, 1992) 101.

6The name, Natangué, of this river is a transcription of the Wolof word naataange, which means prosperity.

7See Goldenstein, Pour lire le roman (Bruxelles: De Boeck-Wesmael, 1988) 75.

8 "Lukács insists on the Hegelian hypothesis according to which the unity of the ancient world – between consciousness and the world, between the Subject and the Object – disappeared" [Lukács insiste sur l'hypothèse hégélienne selon laquelle l'unité du monde antique entre la conscience et le monde, entre le Sujet et l'Objet, a disparu]. See Amadou Koné, Des textes au roman moderne (Frankfurt: Verlag für Interkulturelle Kommunikation, 1993) 21-22.

9See J.M. Bernstein, The Philosophy of the novel (Minneapolis: University of Minneapolis Press, 1984) 57. The author further states: "The central difference between ancient and modern society is that the former is integrated and the latter is problematic." (46).

10[The modern novel] quite simply refuses to tell a story. It is diluted in an incessant verbal flood, or [...] becomes involved in countless directions, totally disorienting the reader [...]: we no longer find the "natural" course of the story to which we are accustomed. [Le roman moderne] renonce tout bonnement à raconter une histoire. [Il] se dilue dans un flot verbal incessant, ou [...] s'engage dans d'innombrables directions et désoriente totalement le lecteur [...]: nous ne retrouvons pas le cours «

naturel » du récit auquel nous sommes habituées]. Goldenstein 10.

11Jean-François Durand analyses at great length Yelli and his followers' quest in his study, "La tradition orale dans le Jujubier du patriarche d'Aminata Sow Fall," See Littératures africaines: Dans quelle(s) langue(s)? (Ivry-sur-Seine: Silex/Nouvelles du Sud, 1997) 93-102.

12See Georges Ngal, Création et rupture en littérature africaine (Paris: L'Harmattan, 1994) 77.

13Jealous of their adopted daughter's economic success, Tacko reminds her of her slave origins.

14This model applies to several types of narratives: "There is indeed the blueprint that governs the tale or the heroic story (Departure-Initiation-Metamorphosis, often accompanied with a return to the starting point) in the novels where traditional thematic is predominant: Initiation and liberation, transition from childhood to adulthood, passage of a state of alienation to freedom." [On retrouve en effet le schéma qui régit le conte ou le récit héroïque (Départ-Initiation-Métamorphose, souvent accompagné de retour au point de départ) dans les romans où domine la thématique traditionnelle: 'initiation et libération, passage de l'état d'enfance à l'état adulte, passage de l'état d'aliénation à la liberté']. See Nora-Alexandra Kazi-Tani, Roman de langue française au Carrefour de l'écrit et de l'oral (Paris: L'Harmattan, 1995) 42-43.

15See Dérive 196. The author also states that for some authors, the novel, even while obeying a variety of conventions, uses particular aspects of a genre of oral tradition. Ibid. 199.

16In her article entitled "Comment définir le genre épique? Un exemple: L'épopée africaine", Seydou identifies the distinctive features of the African epic by compiling a table comparing two types, the West African by Sahelian people, and the Central African by forest people. She concludes by stating that the modes of articulation of meaning and form in African epics can be summarized by three distinctive aspects which are: (1) associating the speech with a specific musical instrument; (2)

the elasticity of the action in the story; and (3) the function of this cultural manifestation. See Christiane Seydou, Journal of The Anthropological Society XIII. 1 (1982): 93.

17The nostalgic return to a glorious past, with the hope of seeing it revived one day, is born and develops in oral epic literature once the conditions [...] of the time had created a climate of general dissatisfaction and discouragement. [Le retour nostalgique vers un passé glorieux, avec l'espoir de le voir revivre un jour, naît et se développe dans la littérature orale épique lorsque les conditions [...] du moment ont créé un climat général d'insatisfaction et de découragement]. See Eno Belinga, Comprendre la literature orale (Issy-les-Moulineaux: Éditions Saint Paul, 1978) 29-30.

18It is the official text that erases the other from the dominant script. See Florence Martin, "Échos et grains de voix dans Le Jujubier du patriarche d'Aminata Sow Fall," French Review 74.2 (2000): 299.

19See Le Jujubier du patriarche 85-86.

20See M. Borgomano, "Le statut de la langue française dans l'oeuvre de Kourouma," Littérature africaines: Dans quelle(s) langue(s)? (Ivry-sur-Seine: Silex/Nouvelles du Sud, 1997) 130.

21The epic does not have for vocation the reproduction for transmittal of an already existing chronological history in a causal sequencing of the facts that constitute it, but rather that of a cultural reinterpretation or, we might say, ideological reinterpretation of the facts. [L'épopée n'a point vocation de reproduire pour la transmettre telle qu'elle fut l'histoire chronologique, dans l'enchaînement causal des faits qui la constituent mais bien plutôt celle d'une réinterprétation culturelle ou, pourrions-nous dire, idéologique des faits]. See Seydou 87.

22See Fréderick Ivor Case, "Littérature traditionnelle et forme romanesque," Éthiopiques 4.3-4 (1987): 50.

23The song, as reconstituted by Aminata Sow Fall, [...] attempts to give a syncretic image of the African past. [Le chant, tel qu'Aminata Sow Fall le reconstitue, [...] s'efforce de donner une image syncrétiste du passé africain]. Durand 95.

24As Dieng and Kesteloot note regarding epics of the same region. See Kesteloot and Dieng 250.

25See Jacques Chevrier, "Présence du mythe dans la littérature africaine contemporaine," in Convergences et divergences dans les littératures francophones, (Paris: l'Harmattan, 1992) 101.

26See Le jujubier du patriarche 111.

27Le Jujubier du patriarche thus answers a question, which had been debated before, on the proper relation between aesthetics and politics. See Thomas Docherty, ed. Postmodernism: A reader (New York: Columbia University Press, 1993) 2-3.

WORKS CITED

Bhabha, Homi. The Location of Culture. New York: Routledge, 1994.

Bernstein, J.M. The philosophy of the Novel. Minneapolis: University of Minneapolis Press, 1984.

Borgomano, M. "Le statut de la langue française dans l'œuvre de Kourouma." Littérature africaines: Dans quelle(s) langue(s)? Actes du Colloque CERPANA Montpellier les 16, 17 et 18 décembre 1994. Ivry-sur-Seine: Silex/Nouvelles du Sud, 1997. 125-134.

Butler, Judith. Gender Trouble: Feminism and the Subversion of Identity. New York: Routledge, 1990.

Case, Frédérick Ivor. "Littérature traditionnelle et forme romanesque." Éthiopiques 4 (1987): 32-52.

Chevrier, Jacques. "Présence du mythe dans la littérature africaine contemporaine." Convergences et divergences dans les littératures francophones: Actes du Colloque 8-9 février 1991. Paris: L'Harmattan, 1992. 92-106.

Derive, Jean. "Style et fiction d'oralité dans la narration de quelques romans francophones." Littératures Francophones : Langues et Styles. Actes du colloque international organisé par Papa Samba Diop. Centre d'Études Francophones. Paris: L'Harmattan, 2001. 191-201.

Diop, Samba. Discours nationaliste et identité ethnique à travers le roman sénégalais. Ivry-sur-Seine: Silex/Nouvelles du Sud, 1999.

Docherty, Thomas, ed. Postmodernism: A Reader. New York: Columbia University Press, 1993.

Durand, Jean-François. "La tradition orale dans Le jujubier du patriarche d'Aminata Sow Fall." Littératures africaines: Dans quelle(s) langue(s)? Actes du Colloque CERPANA Montpellier les 16, 17 et 18 décembre 1994. Ivry-sur-Seine: Silex/Nouvelles du Sud, 1997. 93-102.

Eno Belinga, S.-M. Comprendre la littérature orale africaine. Issy les Moulineaux: Éditions Saint Paul, 1978.

Gilroy, Paul. Against Race: Imagining Political Culture Beyond the Color Line. Cambridge: Harvard University Press, 2000.

Goldenstein, J-P. Pour lire le roman. Bruxelles: De Boeck-Wesmael, 1988.

Halen, Jean. "Les stratégies francophones du style : l'exemple de quelques sauvages du nord." Actes du Colloque International, Littératures Francophones: Langues et Styles. Paris: L'Harmattan, 2001. 213-227.

Hoagarth, Christopher. "Nomadic Francophonie, Francophone Nomads: The case of the Senegalese Novel." Contemporary French and Francophone Studies 10.1 (2006): 55.

Julien, Eileen. African Novels and the Question of Orality. Bloomington: Indiana UP, 1992.

Kazi-Tani, Nora. Roman africain de langue française: au carrefour de l'écrit et de l'oral. Paris: L'Harmattan, 1995.

Kesteloot, Lilyan and Bassirou Dieng. Les épopées d'Afrique noire. Paris: Karthala, 1997.

Kone, Amadou. Des textes au roman moderne. Frankfurt: Verlag für Interkulturelle Kommunikation, 1993.

Martin, Florence. "Échos et grains de voix dans Le Jujubier du patriarche d'Aminata Sow Fall." French Review 74.2 (2000): 296-307.

Ngal, Georges. Création et rupture en littérature africaine. Paris: L'Harmattan, 1994.

Seydou, Christiane. "Comment définir le genre épique ? un exemple : l'épopée africaine." Journal of the Anthropological Society XIII. 1 (1982): 84-98.

Sow Fall, Aminata. L'Appel des arènes. Dakar: NEA, 1982.

– – –. Le Jujubier du patriarche. Dakar: Khoudia, 1993.

Chapter 7
Oral Performance Among the Graffi

NOTES

1Interview conducted at Bambili (informant Adangfung, Quarter head, 60 years old).

2This is an annual festival in the Grass Land of the North West Region in honour of the Gods of the land. It ends with a royal dance.

3The Bali Nyonga people use the Lela festival to honour the gods of the land, war lords, and past heroes of the land.

4Njang performances are very outstanding in the Grass Land. They cover many villages in the North West region of Cameroon, especially the Ngemba villages in the Grass land. It is through the Njang performance that the Grass Landers glorify the past and the present. The content of the Njang song is satirical. The Njang performers also perform in funeral ceremonies. Their principal objective is curbing societal excesses

5They function equally like the Njang performer. They differ at the level of the instruments used and rhythm of their music. The masquerade performers who are present in Njang performance are absent in mbaghulum performances.

6This is the popular traditional regalia used in the Grass field. The different villages that make up the Grass Field have different appellations for this regalia. Tughe is the Bafut language application.

7A shiny moon decoration, usually with a red cloth; a distinguished material attached behind the tughe. It is usually considered as a family title.

8This is the highest title given to women in the Bafut kingdom. It is a round calabash container.

9Its founding fathers were hunters. The mansoh song started as work songs during hunting expeditions, but it is highly organized today. Like the Njang and Mbaghalum songs, it also performs the function of curbing societal excesses.

WORKS CITED

Chukwuma, Helen. Igbo Oral Literature: Theory and Tradition. Port Harcourt: Belpot co., 1994. Print.

Dube, Pamela Z. "Traditional Oral Poetry in New Context: New Direction in South African Performance Poetry?" African Studies Review Vol44, Number 3, December 2001: 64-79. Print.

Klooss, Wolfgang. Across the Lines: Intertextuality and Transcultural Communication in the New Literature in English. Amsterdam-Atlanta: Rodopi, 1998: 93-102. Print.

Finennegan, Ruth. Oral Literature in Africa. Oxford: Oxford U. P., 1970.

Kishani, Bonga Tanla. "On the Interface of Philosophy of Language in Africa: Some Practical and Theoretical Examples". African Studies Review Vol44, Number 3, December 2001: 27-45. Print.

Kofoworola, Ziky& Lateef, Yusef. Hausa Performing Arts and Music. Lagos: Department of Culture, Federal Ministry of Information and Culture, 1987. Print.

Lord, Albert B. The Singer of Tales. London: Harvard U. P., 1960. Print.

Mapanje, Jack & Landeg White eds. Oral Poetry in Africa: An Anthology. New York: Longman, 1983. Print.

Mateso,Locha. La Littérature et sa Critique. Paris: Edition Karthala, 1986. Print.

Nkwi, Paul Nchoji. Traditional Diplomacy: A Study of Inter-Chiefdom Relations in the Western Grass Fields, North Province of Cameroon. Yaounde: The Department of Sociology, 1986. Print.

Okerere, Augustine. "The Performers and Text: Parameters for Understanding Oral Literary Performances."ed. Kloss, Wolfgang in Across the Lines: Intertextuality and Transcultural Communication in the New Literatures in English.Amsterdam-Atlanta:Rodopi, 1988: 37-47. Print.

Okpewho, Isidore.ed. The Oral Performance in Africa. Ibadan: Spectrum Limited,1990. Print.

Olajubu, Oladare. "Yoruba Oral Poetry: Composition and Performance."eds. Abalogu, Uchegbulam N.et als. In Oral Poetry in some Nigerian Communities.Lagos: Nigerian Magazine, Department of Culture, Federal Ministry of Social Development, 1981: 71-85. Print.

Ongoum, Louis-Marie & Celestine Tcheho (eds). Oral Literature in Africa Today: Theoretical and Practical Approaches. Yaounde: CEPER, 1989. Print.

Rosenberg, Bruce A. "Literature and Folklore." Eds. Barricelli & Gibaldi. Interrelations of Literature. New York: Modern Language Association of America, 1982: 90-106. Print.

Sekoni, Ropo. "The Narrator, Narrative- Pattern and Audience Experience of Oral Narrative Performance." Ed. Isidore Okpewho. The Oral Performance in Africa. Ibadan: Spectrum Books Limited, 1990: 139-159. Print.

Soper, et al (eds). Biological Sciences. Cambridge U.P.1984. Print.

Tshibilondi, Albertine Ngoyi. Paradigme de L'interprétation Sémiotique: Esquisse de la Théorie de l'interprétation dans la Semio-Pragmatique de C.S. Pierce. Munich-Kinshasa: Universitaires Africaine, 1997. Print.

Crossing Borders

AGAINST the corruption and devaluation of tradition by imperial cultures Crossing Borders showcases intellectual attempts to commit the process of African interrogation of postcoloniality and postmodernity to the exploration of perspectives on black identities and interactions of contemporary cultural expressions beyond the borders of Africa and across the Atlantic.

We have particularised on theoretical and critical perspectives that reveal how the controversial influence of westernisation of Africa has demanded remedial visions and counteractive propositions to the cycle of abuses and fragmentation of the continent. Our studies of emerging and older works of African artists reveal how the African experience of modernity associated with the western paradigm is fraught with corruption and tensions at various political, social, economic and psychological existence of individuals and nationalities.

We have also distilled some very significant historic and informative insights on modern African and black literary traditions methodically espoused to articulate the greater unity in the diversities, fusions and hybridism that are embedded in the external and subjective realities of our universe.

Our Critical Approaches

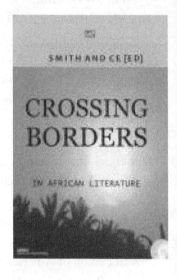

Chin Ce, African writer from Nigeria and author of several books of poetry, critical essays and prose fictions, is editor of the Critical Writing Series on African Literature with Charles Smith, professor of African languages and literature, founder of the Society of African Folklore and fellow of the Literary Society International, LSi.

African Books Network

AFRICAN Books Network with its cosmopolitan outlook is poised to meet the book needs of African generations in times to come.

Since the year 2000 when we joined the information highway of online solutions in publishing and distribution, our African alliance to global information development excels in spite of challenges in the region. Our select projects have given boost to the renaissance of a whole generation of dynamic literature. In our wake is the harvest of titles that have become important referrals in contemporary literary studies. With print issues followed by eContent and eBook versions, our network has demonstrated its commitment to the vision of a continent bound to a common world heritage. This universal publishing outlook is further evidenced by our participation in African Literature Research projects. For everyone on deck, a hands-on interactive is the deal which continues to translate to more flexibility in line with global trends ensuring that African writers are part of the information revolution of the present times.

As one of Africa's mainstream book publishing and distribution networks, writers may look forward to privileged assistance regarding affiliate international and local publishing and distribution service

"Our select projects at African Books Network have given boost to the renaissance of a whole generation of dynamic literature."

Printed in the United States
By Bookmasters